BRIAN T. W. STEWART, CMG
and SAMANTHA NEWBERY

Why Spy?

The Art of Intelligence

HURST & COMPANY, LONDON

To all the gallant men and women who have selflessly, usually unknown and unsung, devoted their lives to intelligence work in the defence of their nation

And to Alexander Wolf Stewart, to whom the future belongs

First published in the United Kingdom in 2015 by
C. Hurst & Co. (Publishers) Ltd.,
41 Great Russell Street, London, WC1B 3PL
© Brian T.W. Stewart and Samantha Newbery, 2015
All rights reserved.
Printed in India

Distributed in the United States, Canada and Latin America by
Oxford University Press, 198 Madison Avenue, New York, NY 10016,
United States of America

The right of Brian T.W. Stewart and Samantha Newbery to be
identified as the authors of this publication is asserted by them
in accordance with the Copyright, Designs and Patents Act, 1988.

A Cataloguing-in-Publication data record for this book
is available from the British Library.

ISBN: 978-1-84904-513-1

www.hurstpublishers.com

This book is printed using paper from registered sustainable
and managed sources.

CONTENTS

CONTENTS

PART THREE

FAMOUS CASES OF INTELLIGENCE IN PRACTICE

PART FOUR

NON-INFORMATION GATHERING INTELLIGENCE
OPERATIONS

ACKNOWLEDGEMENTS

Brian T.W. Stewart, CMG

It is easy to single out the principal people who deserve my heartfelt thanks for persevering and encouraging me along the way in this lengthy operation.

First the members of my family, particularly my long-suffering wife who has lived with *Why Spy?* for over ten years, and with the other slight books that I have published. And Rory too, my son, who read the first drafts with the eye of a professional, successful writer.

Co-equal comes Heather Hooker who, like my family, has been living with *Why Spy?* for many years and has put up uncomplainingly with innumerable changes and additions. Without her help there would have been no book. Next we come to Vice Admiral Le Bailly with whom, although he was fifteen years older than me, I had a magical partnership when I was Secretary of the Joint Intelligence Committee. Sadly he was not able to join me in this book, except by way of a kindly foreword.

Specifically involved in the book in terms of reading drafts and criticising or encouraging, are several academics. Above all stands Professor Eunan O'Halpin of Trinity College Dublin. A friend for many years, he and his pupils passed me relevant material from the cornucopia pro-

ACKNOWLEDGEMENTS

vided by The National Archives in Kew. Without his encouragement I would long since have run out of steam.

Other academics have encouraged me, including Professor R. V. Jones with whom I discussed our subject in the Athenaeum Club in London, long, long ago. I must also name Professor Wang Gungwu, Vice Chancellor of the University of Hong Kong and world-famous historian who said, 'but be careful to suggest that intelligence is not the only factor', and Professor Tony Short and Professor Geoffrey Blainey OA, who kindly read my drafts and made constructive comments.

Then there were distinguished British officers under whom or with whom I served, civil servants, military officers, and diplomats. Men like Sir Gerald Templer, the Tiger of Malaya, Lord MacLehose, Governor of Hong Kong, Lord Trend, Cabinet Secretary, and so on. Lord Carver, once my co-father-in-law, I suspect did not entirely approve of the intelligence profession any more than he approved of the frills and furbelows of the Cavalry (and probably the Highlanders too), but he had a clear view of the uses and limitations of intelligence.

On a personal level I have to thank people like my old (but much younger) friend, Michael Thompson who for decades gave me an anchor in the UK while I continued to roam in China.

There is no satisfactory method for singling out names from the kaleidoscope that has been my life. And I expect that some of my best friends will be happy, as Groucho Marx might have said, 'to be included out', since not everyone wishes to be connected with the business of intelligence.

To those to whom I owe a debt but whose names I have not listed, I offer my apologies, they are not forgotten. Above them all in my post-government life looms a Chinese grandee, His Excellency Mr Jiang Zemin, formerly President of China, who befriended me when I entered China as a fledgling businessman in 1981, and all my other Chinese friends who helped me to understand the mysteries of the Chinese electronic world.

Last, but unique, is Samantha Newbery, my co-author, who joined forces with me when I had all but abandoned ship. Her fresh eye, academic advice and hard work have been invaluable as has her enthusiasm.

BIOGRAPHIES OF THE AUTHORS

Brian T.W. Stewart, CMG (1969)

1940	Worcester College, Oxford.
1942	Commissioned Black Watch.
	School Instructor.
	Action in North West Europe.
1945	Went to Malaya
1946	Retired as Captain; joined Malayan Civil Service.
1947–8	Language student, China.
1949	Employed as Chinese specialist, mostly engaged in intelligence work fighting the terrorists in the local war known as the Malayan Emergency.
1957	Retired as Secretary for Chinese Affairs, Penang.
1957	Joined Foreign Office.
1958–60	Embassy, Rangoon.
1960	British Diplomatic Mission, Beijing.
1961	Consul General Shanghai.
1963–4	Foreign Office, London.
1965–6	Counsellor, British High Commission, Kuala Lumpur.
1967–8	Consul General Hanoi.
1968–72	Secretary of the Joint Intelligence Committee, Cabinet Office.
1973–4	Political Adviser in Hong Kong.
1974–9	Foreign Office; retired.
1979–82	Director of the Rubber Growers' Association, Malaysia.
1982–98	Director of Operations China for Racal Electronics Group.
1998	Retired.

BIOGRAPHIES OF THE AUTHORS

Samantha Newbery

Dr Samantha Newbery is Lecturer in Contemporary Intelligence Studies at the University of Salford, where she has worked since completing her PhD at Trinity College Dublin. Her monograph *Interrogation, Intelligence and Security: Controversial British Techniques* will be published by Manchester University Press in 2015. Her research interests include intelligence ethics, human rights and the prohibition of torture, insurgency and terrorism, policymaking, and Northern Ireland, and she has published on these subjects in the journals *Intelligence and National Security*, *International Politics* and *Irish Studies in International Affairs* as well as in edited books published by Routledge and Edinburgh University Press.

WRITING *WHY SPY?*

Samantha Newbery

Readers may wish to know how this joint book came about and the respective roles of its authors. When I joined Brian on this project in 2011 there was already a draft manuscript which he had been working on spasmodically since retiring in the late 1990s and as he continued to reflect on his own experiences and on the published intelligence literature. The book was a work in progress. I had first met Brian while conducting my doctoral research, through an introduction from Professor Eunan O'Halpin of Trinity College Dublin, when we discussed the use of controversial interrogation techniques in Northern Ireland in 1971 (see Chapter Seven). I accepted Brian's invitation to join the project in order to bring an academic perspective and a fresh eye, and also to identify the terms and episodes of history that, although familiar to him, would need to be explained to younger readers. We have not attempted to produce co-authored material. Where the book presents text in the first person it refers to Brian.

My role has been varied, but has most frequently consisted of providing direction, helping to shape the book, to re-order and edit it, and to turn a first draft into a book that I hope communicates Brian's convictions on the value of intelligence. I have also worked on making *Why Spy?* a book that presents sound arguments, and that will allow readers to enjoy some of the many tales that those who know Brian have been lucky enough to hear first-hand. I also hope that it will be of interest to those who are just starting out on their engagement with published work on intelligence, whether that be because their awareness of intelligence matters has been raised by press coverage of the field or because they are intelligence professionals, as well as to students and scholars of intelligence and of the episodes of history recounted here. It has been a delight to work with Brian on this project, and we have had little difficulty in reaching agreement on how to develop the manuscript into its final form. Playing such a role in turning *Why Spy?* from a draft resting on a shelf into something that will reach a much wider audience has been an honour as well as a role that has brought responsibility. Difficult judgements have had to be made, for instance, on how much background detail to present on the cases addressed in the book. I hope that its finished form does justice to the years of experience and the considered reflections of an intelligence veteran, the majority of whose contributions to the field will remain secret.

There are other members of the *Why Spy?* team whose help I wish to acknowledge. Heather Hooker has played a vital supporting role. Encouragement and advice has been given throughout by Brian's family, by my husband, and by Eunan O'Halpin. Our publisher at Hurst, Michael Dwyer, has also provided valuable support. I am grateful to them all.

FOREWORD

Vice Admiral Sir Louis Le Bailly

Brian Stewart invited me to join forces with him to write this book when he retired from active service in Asia. But I was ninety and my batteries were running low so I volunteered to write this foreword instead.

Brian's career in the Army, Colonial Service, intelligence community, and years on the ground in Malaysia and China, have given him a wide knowledge of the problems of assessing foreign situations and distilling intelligence to the point where it might carry significant weight with politicians.

Both of us agree on the importance of the difficult task; using all sources, attempting to eschew bias, to produce an effective persuasive overview of the world scene.

Brian and I entered an intelligence world that had just been subjected to fundamental changes. As Secretary of a changed Joint Intelligence Committee from 1968, Brian was charged with the duty of providing the great men with the best assessments the Committee could produce. I, on the other hand, looking at the same range of intelligence subjects, found myself handling a team of some 1,000 people. Denis Healey, the

Secretary of State, told me that my job was to build a Defence Intelligence Staff able to tell those who would not listen all the things they did not wish to know.

One thing Brian and I share in common is the perhaps rather arrogant assumption that sometimes we know better than our masters. It is an important bond between us. But as we sat decades later, one in Cornwall, one in Perthshire, we were faced with the Hutton and the Butler Inquiries. It seemed that many of the pillars that had been put in place by the giants of 1968, in an attempt to produce objectivity, had been destroyed.

And then I read a book by Brian's son, Rory, *The Places In Between*, which revealed cold courage and endurance of a quality rarely encountered today. This caused me to write to Brian to congratulate him. And so a friendship, which had lapsed because of his multiplicity of tasks overseas and my increasing dilapidation, has happily been resumed. His battery is still well charged, but mine is getting rather low. However, a flashover may yet take place as his charge brings me the inspiration for which I was once so grateful thirty years ago.

Vice Admiral Sir Louis Le Bailly
Director General Intelligence, 1972–5
December 2009

PREFACE

'The mountains will be in labour and bring forth a ridiculous mouse.'

Horace, *Ars Poetica*, c.13BC

Intelligence is a much more complex affair than most people realise and deserves to be better understood. The media seems to enjoy criticising the doings of the intelligence community and its attempts to retain some modicum of secrecy, without acknowledging that the intelligence community is an important part of our national defence forces and that they need to preserve some secrecy in order to do their job. I hope that my reflections on cases and the methods and machinery of intelligence featured in the book may help readers gain a better understanding of the complexities of an intelligence community, and the problems of maintaining operational security in an age when freedom of information and transparency, and human rights and the rule of law, are dominant words in our democratic society. It will also, I hope, make clear the value of intelligence.

For most of my official life I was engaged in intelligence work. Soon after I landed in Malaya in 1945, I became closely involved with police intelligence as a District Officer when we mounted a campaign to rid the District of the criminal gangs that had filled the vacuum left by the defeated Japanese forces. I learnt the virtues of close collaboration between the civilians and the police. In Singapore, I had a further spell of close collaboration with police intelligence; this time the targets were the secret societies, which were terrifying the public. In 1947 I was posted to Macau to learn Chinese. By the time I returned to Malaya in 1949 the fight (known not as a war but as an Emergency) between the Malayan Communist Party (MCP) and the Government of Malaya was in full swing. From then onwards, I was preoccupied with intelligence related subjects. In 1957 I joined the Foreign Office, and for the next twenty-two years continued to be involved in intelligence matters.

Finally, as an adviser on Chinese Affairs to Western and even Taiwanese businesses trying to capture a share of the Chinese market, I proved to my own satisfaction that experience and open sources can go a long way to producing valid assessments. And I had the satisfaction of pinpointing Jiang Zemin as a possible future leader of China before the corps of China-watchers had noticed him, and produced rather better predictions on China's economic development than most Western observers.

The mountain has taken many years to give birth. As Secretary of the Joint Intelligence Committee (JIC) I wanted to do my homework for my new job, but there seemed to be nothing on the shelves to help. This was a time (1968) when Britain did not even acknowledge the existence of the Secret Intelligence Service (SIS or MI6), and intelligence was so much a taboo subject that the index of such works as Sir Winston Churchill's *History of the Second World War* did not mention the word. My predecessor, Brooks Richards, had already left to become Her Majesty's Ambassador to Greece. So I brooded alone.

The JIC, after the 1968 reforms, seemed to be flying blind as far as knowledge of precedents were concerned. It soon dawned on me that the only person in the Cabinet Office with any broad experience of the management of national intelligence resources was the Secretary of the Cabinet, Sir Burke Trend. The rest of my JIC had earned their spurs in their departments, which were the armed forces, civil departments, and the intelligence agencies. We might have done better had we, collectively, been better trained.

I had the opportunity to persuade the intelligence Knights of the day, who included the heads of the three civilian intelligence agencies known as the Security Service (MI5), SIS and Government Communications Headquarters (GCHQ), that we should commission a historian to look at the subject of intelligence in the Second World War. It did not cause the traditional pillars of secrecy to fall down.

Intelligence is now a subject to be discussed in classrooms and seminars, but the subject is still in its infancy; political biographies and modern histories continue to omit the word intelligence from their indices. Although intelligence studies have now become respectable, we have some way to go before lay people and professionals alike are adequately educated about the strengths, weaknesses, potential and limitations of intelligence and the lessons of history. This book intends to stimulate interest among general readers, as well as the practitioner or serious student of intelligence, and prove a useful introduction to a subject that is not often addressed in its entirety.

There is an increasing amount of literature on intelligence by academics and former officials. This book naturally touches on some of the same subjects, but its perspective is different; one of the authors having spent most of his intelligence career in various roles in the field, not in Whitehall or in academia. Perhaps the most notable of the intelligence books written from 'the inside' is *Intelligence Power in Peace and War* written by another former Secretary of the JIC, and former member of GCHQ, Michael Herman.[1] Also falling into this category is Sir David Omand's *Securing the State*.[2] Omand writes as a former Director of GCHQ and as someone who held the Cabinet Office post of Intelligence and Security Coordinator. Both of these books are well respected by intelligence practitioners, scholars and students alike. Libraries and bookshops also hold useful books that have been produced with a degree of cooperation from the intelligence organisation involved. Professor Christopher Andrew, a highly-regarded intelligence historian, published an authorised history of MI5, *The Defence of the Realm*.[3] This formed part of the UK intelligence community's commemoration of the 100 year anniversary of the founding of the organisation that went on to become MI5 and SIS, a commemoration that also saw Professor Keith Jeffery publish *MI6: The History of the Secret Intelligence Service 1909–1949*.[4] The first volume of Michael S. Goodman's official history of the JIC was published in 2014,[5] and Professor Richard Aldrich, another respected intelligence scholar, has published a history of GCHQ.[6] There are, of course, other quality books on aspects of intelligence that result from the research of these and other distinguished academics.

Why Spy? discusses the intelligence machinery, methods of collecting intelligence, assessment of raw intelligence material, and the misuse and abuse of intelligence. It also draws attention to the need to go behind the simple headline 'intelligence failure' and identify the responsible culprits who may well be policymakers or military commanders, rather than intelligence officers. It contains analyses of cases that further highlight the value of intelligence and the pitfalls that can be encountered. Intelligence has no magic wand; the judgements made by intelligence practitioners and the policymakers who receive their material render it an art not a science. Those individuals with experience as practitioners who have read this book's reflections have all found something interesting in it and do not consider its views outlandish.

It will, I hope, help all interested in the subject of intelligence to consider the wider issues, which inevitably are scantily covered in the press, or even in official inquiries. I hope it will stimulate greater understanding and help readers to recognise the complexities of the scene. It is a book providing reflections and thoughts on intelligence that I wish had been available to me when I joined the JIC. While it may be difficult to find the time to conduct broad reading on intelligence cases and problems, a little intelligence history is a valuable asset, whether the reader is in the intelligence business or not. The examples discussed highlight the pitfalls of the past.

The short answer to 'why spy?' is 'in order to discover the truth behind the lies, and obfuscations of our rivals and our enemies.' There is an important, current, subsidiary question: 'is the growing cost justified?' Some senior members of government and its institutions who receive material from the intelligence agencies suggest that secret intelligence is only useful to confirm that their conclusions are correct. Yet the chapters in this book provide examples where timely intelligence has been a significant ingredient in success, helping commanders to victory and reducing the 'butcher's bill'. The value of intelligence, and of practising and using it well, are the central themes of *Why Spy?*

INTRODUCTION

Liars, deceivers, eavesdroppers, covert surveillance operators, thieves, burglars, lockpickers, perhaps kidnappers or even assassins. Such are some of the roles that may be required of an intelligence officer or a secret agent. On the other hand the work may consist only of humdrum administrative activities. The intelligence officer's services to the state cannot be publicly recognised, but may entail serious danger, and often long unsocial hours. So why are people prepared to devote their lives to intelligence, a profession that provides a conveniently silent scapegoat when there is a failure, but cannot be publicly congratulated on success? Is intelligence work important? Indeed, is it of much use at all if—as so often is the case—it is ignored or misused?

Fortunately there are still enough people prepared to spend their lives on intelligence work. Intelligence, despite the nature of what it involves, is an honourable profession, staffed by honourable patriots. Like the soldier trained to be an assassin in the line of duty, the spy is trained to steal and to bug to protect the state. Secret intelligence work is not for the faint hearted, but it is an essential weapon in the armoury of any major nation. Even Secretary of State Henry Stimson of the US, who objected after the First World War to proposals to create a US intelligence agency with the remark, '[g]entlemen do not read other people's mail', changed his view after the Japanese surprise attack at Pearl Harbor in 1941 (see Chapter Eight).

It is often suggested that prostitution is the oldest profession in the world. But from the dawn of history people have been seeking to discover the intentions and secrets of their enemies; to penetrate the secu-

1

rity barriers behind which their enemies work. Today the West faces well-funded international terrorist groups and threats to cyber-security. So long as our imperfect world exists there will continue to be a need for intelligence services to seek the truth behind what Churchill called the bodyguard of lies. *Why Spy?* is concerned with the eternal verities and basic problems which always have, and always will, be a part of intelligence work.

The US's Central Intelligence Agency (CIA) has emblazoned above its front hall the motto, '[a]nd ye shall know the truth and the truth shall make you free', emphasising that the search for the truth is the central function of intelligence. Yet intelligence is not a science, and it has no crystal ball. The job of intelligence is to do its best to find the truth and report findings without selectivity or embroidery, however unpalatable they may be.

The intelligence agencies' customers, whether they be elected representatives of the people, civil servants or members of the armed forces, must accept that intelligence, like any other form of human activity, has limitations. It can no more predict the future with absolute certainty than an economist or an investment adviser. It can record the facts discovered, suggest near certainties, probabilities and possibilities. It can be held to account to tell the truth, the whole truth, and nothing but the truth, but it can only offer a best guess, based on all the available information.

In the fifth century BC, a number of Chinese generals produced a book called *The Art of War* (*Bing Fa*), which they attributed to a general called Sun Tzu. *The Art of War*, almost certainly the earliest book written on intelligence, is adamant about the crucial importance of intelligence. It says that 'a General who is too stingy to spend generously on intelligence is not fit to be called a General.' *The Art of War*'s principles of intelligence remain as valid today as they were in the fifth century BC.

Many successful leaders have shared this view on the importance of intelligence. Thousands of years later Niccolò Machiavelli showed an enthusiasm for intelligence that matched that of Sun Tzu. The Duke of Wellington, soldier and politician, emphasised the need to know what was happening on the other side of the hill. George Washington, the first President of the US, who spent 10 per cent of his budget on intelligence, wrote, '[t]he necessity of procuring good intelligence is apparent and need not be further urged'. General Dwight D. Eisenhower, who went on to be President of the US, paid effusive compliments to intelligence for its contribution to Allied victory in the Second World War and to the saving of many servicemen's lives. One eminent historian, Sir Harry Hinsley, considered that the Allied successes in reading the German signals shortened the Second World War by three years. Churchill was an avid consumer of intelligence throughout the war.

But not everyone agrees. The renowned military thinker Carl von Clausewitz said 'most intelligence is false.' US President Lyndon B. Johnson commented when intelligence challenged his view of the Vietnam War that those intelligence fellows reminded him of a cow he used to milk, which would swish its tail across the milk pail if he were not careful. As Secretary of the JIC, I had a ringside seat from which to observe the machinery of the Anglophone nations. The late Sir Reginald Hibbert, a close friend from my undergraduate days at Oxford, and a distinguished Foreign Office mandarin argued that the principal value of secret intelligence was to confirm his assessments. This view seemed to me to be close to 'don't confuse me with the facts, my mind is made up already.' It is, of course, a view shared by others that intelligence is troublesome if it challenges the received wisdom. It has been well said that customers sometimes use intelligence as a drunk uses a lamp post: for support not illumination. In the main, however, the value of good intelligence and the worth of their intelligence professionals have been recognised by western leaders.

Definitions of Terms

Discussions on intelligence are bedevilled by language problems. For example, the Japanese 'joho' and the Chinese 'qingbao' mean both intelligence in the sense that we use the word in the name Joint Intelligence Committee, and information as in Ministry of Information. The world is full of languages which use the same words for both intelligence and information.

This book adopts the following conventions:

Intelligence: the business of collecting information, analysing it, assessing it, and presenting it to those known as customers to assist their policymaking and decisions. This activity is not, of course, the exclusive domain of governments; any organisation needs a good information base.

Information: the raw material upon which intelligence is based.

Secret: something hidden physically or concealed by, for example, the use of a cipher.

Secret intelligence: information derived through covert, clandestine activity to discover the truth behind the deceits and obfuscations offered to the general public.

Strategic intelligence: the big picture, current and future, based on all sources of intelligence.

Tactical or operational intelligence: something of immediate concern related to a specific event, not the broad or longer term picture.

Open source or overt intelligence: the whole gamut of material made available to the public through all types of publications, the media, radio broadcasts, public records, and the internet.

Agents: The CIA calls its officers agents. In the UK the term is normally used to mean a person who, on behalf of an intelligence service and directed by an intelligence officer, carries out clandestine tasks. *Why Spy?* adopts the British usage.

Case officer: The individual responsible for a particular case and for the agent concerned. They run the agents, brief and debrief them, pay them and control them.

Staff officer: An officer who is not in command, but assists commanders to ensure that their plans are carried out effectively.

The definition of spy in particular is of more than semantic interest: authoritarian regimes, such as the government of the former Soviet Union, have bizarre views on what constitutes spying. In China in the 1960s a foreign banker was charged with the crime of espionage because, like foreign representatives around the world, he studied the local situation and sent press cuttings to his head office. He was jailed for two years.

Such countries lump together diplomats, defence attachés, intelligence officers, and journalists as spies, since all share the irritating habit of studying and commenting on the local scene. Only the more sophisticated governments will distinguish between the defence attaché, a licensed overt intelligence gatherer, the intelligence officer, a covert intelligence gatherer, the diplomat lying perhaps but not spying for their country, and the news reporter with freedom to roam and ask too many questions.

The Kim Philby case reminds us of differing perspectives. Philby became the most well-known member of the Cambridge Five spy ring who were recruited while studying at Cambridge University before the Second World War and who spied for the Soviet Union during the Cold War. To most Britons and particularly to former colleagues in the British intelligence community, Philby was perceived as a vile traitor who had sent many brave people to a gruesome fate at the hands of the KGB, the Soviet Union's principal Cold War intelligence agency. But to the KGB, Philby was a hero whom they decorated and rewarded generously for his treachery.

Just as the guerrilla triad might read 'I am a freedom fighter, you are a guerrilla, he is a terrorist', the intelligence triad might read 'I am an intelligence officer, you are an agent, he is a spy'. Although the word spy is more often than not used pejoratively, for our purposes in Britain, and in this book, the definition of spy and agent are the same. They are people who, conscious of their intelligence role, have been recruited to carry out an intelligence task.

Structure of the Book

This book reflects on the broad body of intelligence work: the roots of intelligence failure, the complexity of organisation and multiplicity of methods, and the wide variety of people involved. It also looks at related subjects such as ethics, deception and Special Operations. To do so, the book is organised into four parts. The first concerns three cases in which I was involved during my working life. The Malayan Emergency started with a dismal failure of intelligence, and ended with the creation of an excellent intelligence machine. The security forces (the military and the police) were no longer the ambushed but the ambushers. The Vietnam War illustrates the point that intelligence alone is of limited use if there are no effective government security forces for it to support. The Chinese discussion demonstrates a different point. High level secret sources were not required: travelling around the country, for instance, provided a way to collect useful intelligence.

The second addresses the components of the intelligence machine and what can be described as the core activities carried out by intelligence agencies: collecting intelligence material and assessing it. Coordinating so complex a machine must be attempted but, as explained in Chapter Four, we should be realistic. The list of types of intelligence collection methods in Chapter Five is not exhaustive but includes methods new to the published literature on intelligence, while Chapter Six identifies the common fallacies of the intelligence assessment process. Chapter Seven discusses the moral dilemmas raised by intelligence practices, including the tension sometimes observable between what is effective and what is permissible.

The third part of the book addresses seminal cases in which I was not directly involved but had the opportunity to discuss with those who were. Pearl Harbor, and the Cuban Bay of Pigs and Missile Crisis cases, have all been covered in considerable depth officially and so provide a great deal more detail on the work of an intelligence community than is usually available to the public. These cases illustrate many of the important lessons discussed in this book. The Pearl Harbor disaster was a victory for the Japanese operationally in respect of intelligence and security, although they underestimated the will and ability of the United States to retaliate. Its intelligence customers and military commanders did not fare well in the investigations that followed. The Bay of Pigs was an unmitigated catastrophe operationally and from the intelligence viewpoint, while the Cuban Missile Crisis was nearly a disaster, even though intelligence was a significant ingredient in its ultimate success. The British government's misuse of intelligence relating to Iraqi Weapons of Mass Destruction (WMD) in the run up to the 2003 war in Iraq has also seen relatively large amounts of information enter the public domain and highlighted the difficulties that can arise in the relationship between intelligence and policy. Together, these and the cases in Part One illustrate many of the lessons drawn out in the analyses of the intelligence machine and of the collection and assessment of intelligence. Each case illustrates that no matter how effective the analysis or brilliant the collection work, such efforts are wasted, unless the intelligence agency concerned can transform the raw material into accurate and timely reports that directly impact its customer.

The final part of the book addresses operations conducted to influence events, including the difficult and as yet unresolved question of who should run and carry out Special Operations, the prerequisites for successful deception operations such as those carried out during the Second World War that gave Allied forces the strategic advantage, and shaped western intelligence services' attitudes to assassination. By focusing on the nature of the intelligence business *Why Spy?* addresses the fundamental question of why intelligence is important.

The rules of good intelligence work may be crystallised into the following ten commandments, which are expanded upon and illustrated in the chapters that follow:

1. Report nothing but the unvarnished and, as far as possible, the whole truth. Understand, but do not pander to, the prejudices and preconceptions of the customer.

2. The future: remind customers that intelligence officers cannot see in to the future; they can only make educated guesses about what it might consist of.

3. Assessment of intelligence material: beware of intellectual laziness, mirror imaging, prejudice, racial or professional arrogance, bias, groupthink, and the sin of assuming that the future will develop, broadly speaking, along the same lines as the past.

4. People are more important than organisations: top priority should be given to the recruitment of high quality candidates.

5. Agents: beware of the possibilities of exaggeration, deception, and a desire to please the case officer.

6. Liaison: remember that friends, whether they be domestic or abroad, have hidden agendas.

7. Validation: do not allow an agent's case officer to be the sole judge of the validity of the agent's reporting.

8. Sources: secret and official sources have no monopoly of the truth. Open, readily accessible, sources are also important.

9. Intelligence requirements: prune these vigorously as no service can cover every subject.

10. State of grace: ensure that you are flexible in your response to the unexpected, which by definition has not been envisaged in the list of national intelligence requirements.

PART ONE

THREE ASIAN CASES

THE MALAYAN EMERGENCY

AN INTELLIGENCE SUCCESS STORY

'The British have already created a totalitarian, complete penetrating system of administration from Federal Government to small town and Malay villages... there is no weak link in the enemy's administration for us to exploit.'

MCP directive, December 1948

'I would not dispute that the enemy's intelligence effort improved under Templer's direction.'

Chin Peng, former Secretary General of the MCP, 2003

'The Malayan Emergency was an exemplar of counter-insurgency, and those who participated have every right to be proud. The greatest credit must go to the people of Malaya who made great personal sacrifices, saw with sound sense where their real interests lay and employed considerable political skill, imagination and restraint in attaining their ends...and General Templer was the man-of-the-hour.'

Field Marshal The Lord Carver

'When at an impressionable age you have to remove a pig spear from the stomach of a rubber tapper pinned to a tree by the spear and left to die a lingering agonising death, or pick up the bodies of two Chinese miners executed in front of their families by "elimination" squads as "running dogs" by driving eight inch nails through their foreheads, one has little affection for those responsible.'

Sergeant Gus Fletcher, former Malayan Police Officer

I first arrived in Malaya, now Malaysia, in 1945. It was my first Asian posting, my first love, where I cut my intelligence teeth, and where I spent the best part of twenty years of my life. I have no difficulty in remembering, with exceptional clarity, my introduction to Asia as a member of the British Military Administration (BMA). I travelled from Singapore to Penang by train. After four days, we arrived late at night at Butterworth Station, from where I crossed on the ferry to Penang. Next morning, after sleeping on the jetty, I set off on an ex-Japanese miniature torpedo boat to Pulau Jerejak, the pre-war immigration station, now converted into a refugee camp, and which became my sole responsibility.

Subsequently, as District Officer Bukit Mertajam—a job usually held by an experienced Malayan Civil Service officer in his late thirties—I was helped by an exceptionally patient Malay Chief Clerk, and kindly Malay headmen who guided me through local custom. One issue bothered me: law and order. The leaders of the District grumbled that there had been no crime whilst Malaya was in Japanese hands during the Second World War. This was hardly surprising since we did not practise the system of summary justice favoured by the Japanese military, but I was incensed. The local Senior Police Officer agreed to pool all our resources and with ambushes day and night, we soon persuaded the bandits to mend their ways or go elsewhere. This was my first and highly satisfying experience of the force multiplying effect of close collaboration between civil authority and uniformed services.

By the time I returned to Malaya in 1949 the country was aflame; the insurgents, known as Communist-Terrorists (CTs), seemed to be winning. Despite their advances, we turned the tables and it was highly satisfactory to be involved in close collaboration with the military and the police in the successful recovery of the situation. This chapter derives first and foremost from my experiences there.

I was technically an Administrative Officer but because I knew two dialects of Chinese I found myself fully occupied in support of the security forces who by and large did not know any Chinese. I was collector, assessor, and operations man all rolled into one. My activities included raising private funds for the building of decent Chinese schools, publishing a Chinese newspaper, acting as the private secretary to the leader of the Chinese community in Malaya, and advising General Sir Gerald Templer, Malaya's High Commissioner and Director of Operations. My objectives were to persuade the Malayan Chinese that we were on their side, and to persuade the terrorists that they could not win and should surrender and work with us. I was more what the Indian Civil Service would have called a 'Political' than an Administrator.

The Emergency[1]

The victory of the Malayan government over the communist insurgents was a unique event in South East Asia. Elsewhere the communists won, and the West departed. In Malaya the government won, and we stayed to help our friends after independence. But that is not the reason for including this case in the book; it has been included because it provides a clear example of the importance of good intelligence in such a situation. There are intelligence lessons that ought to be learned from the Malayan case and that can aid efforts to tackle insurgents elsewhere, even though every case will be different: the recipe which worked so well in Malaya could not be used effectively in the very different circumstances of Vietnam. Nonetheless, analysis of the Malayan case draws attention to valuable intelligence lessons. At the onset of the Emergency the British general in command complained bitterly that his patrols were looking for will-o'–the-wisps, and all too often weary soldiers returned from two weeks of misery in the jungle having made no contact with the enemy. The situation changed dramatically as the intelligence machine improved. At the beginning of the Emergency they ambushed us. When the new, strong, trained Special Branch (SB) was in full swing, we ambushed them.

The Malayan Emergency started in June 1948 and officially ended in 1960. The government's Emergency Regulations were a response to the terrorist activities of members of the MCP, an illegal organisation founded in 1935, and which survived the war, despite Japanese efforts, to enjoy legal status under the changed post-war conditions. In fact their first shots were fired by mavericks who jumped the gun before the MCP had decided to launch the insurgency, but soon Malaya was aflame with ambushes on roads, attacks on estates, assassinations, torture, and intimidation of the rural, especially the Chinese and Indian, communities.

The British official connection with Malaya and Singapore dated from the end of the eighteenth century when the two semi-deserted islands lying at the north and the south of the Malacca Straits, first Penang and then Singapore, were acquired by treaty from the Malay

13

Sultans. In 1824 Malacca, acquired by treaty from the Dutch, became the third of the Straits Settlements. All the Malay States became British protectorates; some federated, others unfederated, with British advisers alongside the Sultans.

The plantations and mines on the peninsula flourished, supported by the ports of Singapore and Penang. This conglomerate was, by most standards, a paradise due to a benign climate and good soil. But economic development had been accompanied by a considerable influx of Chinese and Indians. It was a plural society, where the Malays were still in the majority, their lands and customs protected by law, but also there was growing jealousy of the Chinese and Indian immigrants who had moved up the social and economic ladder.

This paradise was rudely awakened in December 1941, when the Japanese launched their air and sea armadas to attack the Western powers in East Asia. Although the attack on Pearl Harbor was only a partial success, in a matter of weeks Malaya and the allegedly impregnable fortress of Singapore were in Japanese hands, and most of the British were in prison. The Japanese occupation of 1941–5 brought massacres and misery to the Chinese, too, and the brutality of the Japanese Army and its notorious intelligence arm, the Kempeitai, ensured that whatever the Malayans thought of the British they preferred British colonialism to Japanese colonialism. I felt warmly welcomed when I arrived in autumn 1945 as part of the British Military Administration (BMA).

On 1 April 1946, the BMA ended, handing over to Sir Edward Gent, home civil servant from the Colonial Office who was largely responsible for the production of the new Malayan Union constitution. The Malays condemned the constitution for giving too many rights to the immigrants; the Sultans stayed away from the airport greeting ceremony, and soon the Colonial Office was drafting a different constitution. In 1948 the Colonial Office's new constitution was introduced. This replaced the Union with a Federation, and removed proposals for granting citizenship to non-Malays.

Almost immediately the Malayan Communist Party (MCP) started their terrorist activities; on 4 July Gent, flying back for consultations in Whitehall, was killed when his plane crashed. He was succeeded in October 1948 by Sir Henry Gurney, an experienced Colonial Officer from Palestine; three years later he was killed in a terrorist ambush.

When, in February 1952, General Templer arrived to take command as High Commissioner and Director of Operations morale in Malaya was at a low ebb. I had the privilege of working with him. Armed with a political brief to hasten independence, and Churchill's backing, Templer made a rapid improvement in morale, as the security forces and intelligence from a greatly enlarged and well trained SB began to turn the tables on the terrorists. We were ambushing them, and by August 1957, when Malaya became independent, few active terrorists remained; the rest had retreated over the border to Thailand, or been killed, died in the jungle, been captured or had seen the light and surrendered.

Determinants of Success

Success in Malaya owed a great deal to good intelligence, the psychological warfare (psywar) campaign to win the support—the 'hearts and minds'—of the rural population, and the programme of resettlement to New Villages to deny the CTs support from the rural communities they had intimidated.

In 1948 the brunt of the Emergency was borne in the countryside by the police, planters and miners. Rural Chinese suspected to be collaborating with the government all came within the communist rubric, 'running dogs of the colonialist imperialist aggressors'. The police were seriously hampered by a lack of Chinese-speaking officers to handle agents and debrief CTs, captured or surrendered. I had the task of establishing a Chinese Language School to remedy this deficiency. By 1952 the intelligence situation had been transformed: there was a growing stable of good agents, a solid analytical base, considerable knowledge of the CTs' methods, organisation and personalities, and a useful number of Chinese-speaking officers to help to build a bridge to the Chinese community. One lesson learned was the need to protect agents from their own folly: in one case a highly productive agent insisted on a large cash payment despite the warnings of his case officer of the danger of being betrayed by high spending. Within a month he was dead.

By the early 1950s the initiative no longer lay with the MCP. Security force numbers had increased drastically: police jungle squads had been formed, and tens of thousands of Special Constables had been recruited to guard rural townships, estates and mines. But without the aid of SB intelligence the enemy would still have been able to strike with impunity in rural areas and prove next to impossible to find in the jungle.[2] The increasing flow of good intelligence enabled us to disrupt the supply system and to hamper the CTs' attempts to contact and intimidate the rural Chinese. The rural population were resettled into defended New Villages, food control and curfews were put into place, preventing the rural Chinese passing food and other supplies to the CTs and hampering the CTs' ability to coerce the local inhabitants. These and the other measures adopted were part of the success. Meanwhile there had been a vast expansion of the police and considerable reinforcement on the military front, accompanied by the development of jungle warfare training that helped the security forces cope with the unfamiliar tropical environment.

When independence came in 1957, the MCP and its guerrilla forces were no longer a serious threat. Intelligence had certainly played a major role in the victory, not only in the collection, analysis and coordination of intelligence, but also in policymaking. By 1957, we knew more about the organisation, order of battle (ORBAT), and the people in the so-called Malayan People's Liberation Army (the military arm of the MCP), than the Secretary General of the MCP, skulking across the border in Thailand.

The Malayan victory over the CTs continues to be cited in military intelligence schools as a textbook case of how to make the best use of intelligence to defeat terrorism and insurgency. However, there were some elements which contributed to victory that were unique to the time and place, and this should, naturally, be borne in mind when seeking to transfer its lessons to present and future conflicts. Malaya was a British Colonial Protectorate and the government acted quickly and decisively through chief executives at State and District level. British parliamentarians were critical of General Templer's dictatorial ways, and would have been more critical had they known of the speed with which the colonial administrators, with the support of the State War Executive Committees (SWECs), could make decisions.

The central strength of the Malayan system, perhaps a unique strength, was the fusion, under Templer, of all branches of government in a combined effort. Templer, High Commissioner, Director of Operations, and intelligence aficionado, made it clear to everyone—military, civilian, political or commercial—that they were expected to help. This appears in the British Army's 2009 Counter-Insurgency Field Manual in the form of a requirement for 'unity of effort' involving all the instruments of state working together for a common end.

One of the determinants of success was the State War Executive Committees (SWECs), which operated at national and district levels across Malaya. They included representatives from the civil service, police, SB, military, and Chinese Affairs. Although I was not on the SWECs, I had the right to attend at all levels and speak when I wanted to. A particular strength was the opportunity they provided for a weekly pooling of intelligence and ideas. In their intelligence assessment role they did, at local level, what large national machines seem to find so hard—to exchange information and views from all sources and bury their disagreements and departmental biases in order to arrive at useful, positive conclusions.

Templer was a great supporter of the Chinese Secretariat in which I worked and which contributed to intelligence success in Malaya. In 1953, at my suggestion, the Central District of Malacca was designated as a 'white area', and excused from the curfews, food controls and other inconveniences of the Emergency Regulations, on the alleged grounds that the citizens of Central Malacca were cooperating so loyally. It was not difficult to persuade Templer that the experiment would cost nothing, that the local CTs would not be sure whether the story was true or false, and that other Districts might be encouraged to become more supportive of government. The bluff worked and by the time that Malaya became independent most Districts had been declared 'white'.

General Templer had three major objectives: intelligence, reorganisation of the police, and public relations. All were rapidly achieved. There have been those who downplay the importance of Templer's role in the victory, citing the fact that the plan for resettlement and all the Emergency Regulations that helped to undermine the communist organisation had been drafted before his arrival. However, without the leadership that he provided, the plan drawn up by General Sir Harold Briggs, the previous Director of Operations, to separate the CTs from the rest of the population would not have had the same, beneficial results; his enthusiastic support for every sort of intelligence, and for every form of hearts and minds work, particularly in winning the cooperation of the Chinese population, was a vital contribution to victory in Malaya. Templer's achievements demonstrate that individuals working within intelligence organisations can be highly influential.

The Pre-Emergency Failure of Intelligence

The intelligence situation at the start of the Emergency was a far cry from that which was developed in the following years. The failure of the

Malayan Security Service (MSS) to recognise the growing communist threat prior to 1948 seems to have stemmed as much from a lack of intelligence experience among the senior customers, as to a lack of assessment experience among the professionals. Neither the customers, in this case the civil heads—Commissioner General of Singapore, Governor of Singapore and High Commissioner of Malaya—nor their military colleagues had any relevant experience of intelligence; and so they did not know the right questions to ask of their intelligence chief, nor understand his urgent need for more staff and greater expertise.

The minute summarised in this chapter's Appendix B reflects the fact that none of the customers ever asked for a focussed threat assessment. There was no complaint that the MSS's fortnightly Intelligence Summary (Appendix B) was little more than an undigested situation report (sitrep). None of the customers are on record as asking for comment on the implications for South East Asia of the growing strength of the communist movement in Asia and above all in China where it seemed almost certain that the nationalists were about to be driven out by the communists.

Those who would argue that these weaknesses were not the fault of these customers should remember that these professionals, from Colonel John Dalley, Director of the MSS, downwards, had no general intelligence training; they were colonial police officers doing their best, possibly excellent at investigating serious crime but certainly without the experience of their equivalents in India. The very title of the organisation, MSS, tells its own tale. Their brief was narrow; security, not intelligence. Dalley was not even allowed to become a member of the Joint Intelligence Committee Far East, on the grounds that he might take too parochial a view of the committee's purposes.

Had Loi Tak, our star secret agent, remained Secretary General of the Communist Party, it would not have greatly mattered that the assessment machinery was inadequate. Loi Tak's reporting would have kept the British adequately informed of the plans of the MCP; he might even have been able to persuade his colleagues that the time was still not ripe for an armed confrontation with the British. Once Loi had left in March 1947, British intelligence was unsighted: it was a horrible example of being over-reliant on a single source of intelligence.

In neighbouring Vietnam and Indonesia, nationalism was the principal driving force behind the insurrections led by Ho Chi Minh and

Bung Soekarno respectively. But the Malayan insurgency was the child, not of Malay nationalism, but of Chinese resident in Malaya. Further to a lack of experience in intelligence assessment, the appendices to this chapter also demonstrate a lamentable absence of urgency within the ranks of the Malayan and Singapore officials during the period of 1946 to 1948. The Commissioner General's Committee was afloat in a sea of ignorance and the MSS, undermanned and under trained, did not offer a clear threat assessment. The affairs of the MCP, which almost entirely consisted of Chinese members, seldom rated more than a paragraph in the MSS's fortnightly Political Intelligence Journal, although in China the communists were thrashing the armies of the nationalist government. When I was in China as a language student, I did not need any intelligence training or secret sources to work out that the communists were winning, and it should not have been difficult to recognise that communists throughout Asia would be encouraged by events in China.

The appendices below demonstrate a poor performance by all concerned. Fortunately the MCP was small, inexperienced, and badly led, giving the Malayan Government time to reform and improve its intelligence machine. Neither the Commissioner General nor his Committee probed the assessments, such as they were, and the MSS Political Intelligence Journal (Appendix B) was little more than a scrapbook.

Appendix A: Summary of the Commissioner General's Conference, 26 June 1947

This meeting of June 1947 shows that it was not only Dalley, Director of the MSS, who failed to appreciate the magnitude of the danger posed by communism. The Commissioner General, Malcolm Macdonald, refused to recommend that the MCP should be banned as it had been before the war, and he and his colleagues failed to press Dalley for a fresh threat assessment. The record conveys little sense of urgency, the need to help the MSS to get staff or, indeed, of any understanding of the fundamental flaws in the intelligence machine.

The meeting was attended by the High Commissioner of Malaya and Governor of Singapore, their Secretaries for Chinese Affairs (SCAs), their senior officers in each of the armed services, the Director MSS, the Trade Union Adviser and representatives of the Foreign Office and Security Service. Macdonald said that he had called the meeting in order to discuss communism. He considered that, '[c]ommunism was Enemy no. 1 in these territories. It was a serious enemy and capable of becoming a formidable one. Without falling into the error of exaggeration or excitement it had to be realised that communism would have to be dealt with in a pretty big and effective way in Malaya and Singapore.' He outlined the strengths of the communists, describing their tentacles throughout society. It was his personal view that 'it was very necessary to have a very strong and coherent policy to counteract the activities of the Communists.'

Gent said that he did not think that Macdonald's statement was exaggerated, and thought that the government needed the opinion of experts to identify weaknesses and to show them how they could be countered. Dalley reported on the state of the MCP and its links with international communism. Macdonald presumed that '[t]he Communists' aim was to get rid of the government.' Dalley agreed.

During subsequent discussion Dalley agreed with Macdonald that the MCP was Chinese dominated and its strength lay in the support of Chinese population of the two territories. The SCA Malaya remarked that although the Kuomintang (KMT), China's ruling party, were still strong in Malaya they were losing the war in China, and if the communists won then KMT influence would be correspondingly reduced in Malaya.

The Commander in Chief, Far East, did appear to appreciate the seriousness of the threat. He asked why the subversive trade unions and the Communist Party were not outlawed? Where was the British answer to countering international communism? In his opinion the KMT were a worse menace than the MCP.[3] Macdonald replied that the British democratic tradition tolerated communists as well as democrats and, therefore, Westminster would not be prepared to authorise the proscription of the MCP unless it could be proved categorically that it was engaged in a criminal conspiracy. Gent, pointing out that the MCP had been proscribed before the war, asked why was it impossible to go back to the pre-war policy. The communists were training hundreds while we were training only a handful in Britain to counter subversion. Macdonald wondered whether the KMT could not be used to help counter communism in the Chinese community. The SCA Malayan Union vigorously opposed this idea and was supported by Dalley, who described the corrupt and vicious nature of the KMT.

The meeting discussed the importance of a healthy development of democratic institutions. The Trade Union Adviser said that he wished that the Malays would act more vigorously like a proper party. Macdonald however thought that Dato' Onn had made a good start and that his United Malays National Organisation, a political party, would develop effectively. Macdonald suggested that support should be sought among the leading Chinese business people but the Trade Union Adviser warned against reliance on support from the Towkay (business) class. In his view the middle class clerks of all races were more likely to provide a solid base.

Macdonald initiated a discussion on the MSS's requirements. Dalley said that he needed all the help he could get from agencies outside Malaya since much of the impetus for subversion and training came from outside.[4] Macdonald raised the question of shortages of trained intelligence staff since the Malaya and Singapore governments could not spare enough people to satisfy the needs of the MSS. He suggested that he and the two governments should work together on the problem of recruiting staff from outside Malaya. Gent did not support this idea and talked of the need to resolve constitutional matters before embarking on any programme of recruitment from outside the Malayan Police. Macdonald suggested that Dalley should consult with the Whitehall security and intelligence representatives and if manpower could be found, no doubt finance could also be found. This suggestion also failed to find favour with Gent. The matter, in his view, should first be considered by the Malaya and Singapore Commissioners of Police and the Director of MSS, so as to agree on a required establishment. Gent preferred to prioritise maintaining constitutional niceties over creating an effective intelligence machine. While the threat from the MCP and weaknesses in the MSS were acknowledged by the attendees of this meeting, they were not fully appreciated.

Appendix B: The MSS Political Intelligence Journal

The first of this fortnightly series appeared on 30 April 1946. The last issue is dated 30 August 1948. The series therefore covered the months immediately before, and the first six-weeks of, the Emergency. Dalley had been complaining regularly about a lack of staff in the MSS, and the quality of the Journal reflects this shortage.

The Journal was about the nuts and bolts of organisations, and provided sitreps. It was padded out from time to time with a Who's Who list of the great and the bad. The format was unsuited to busy senior customers of intelligence, and unlikely to have much impact on policy. Senior customers were, in effect, left to make their own assessments.

The Journal never produced anything remotely resembling a threat assessment, but neither Dalley nor his customers worried about this. The defect could have been remedied by a small team of skilled assessors or an interdepartmental committee to bring together intelligence from all sources into a general assessment. It took the declaration of the Emergency to focus attention on this weakness.

Until mid-1948 most of the material in the Journal was concerned with Asian nationalism: Indonesian, Malay, Indian and Chinese. On the Chinese front, it was the nationalists, not the communists, who were the focus of MSS coverage until 1948. The KMT had long been the bugbear of the governments of Malaya and Singapore: a malign influence encouraging Malayan Chinese to give their loyalty not to Malaya but to mother China, and a group seriously tarnished by corruption and close relations with Triads (secret societies) and their criminal activities. So it was the threat of the KMT, not the communists, which concerned senior Malayan officials. Although the overt satellites of the MCP were regularly covered in some detail in the MSS Journal, the MCP itself never rated more than a few lines until the Emergency was declared.

This imbalance probably reflected a paucity of sources capable of covering the MCP. The overt satellites: trade unions, China Democratic League, Chinese teachers and stevedores were softer targets, and such matters as developments in China and the structure of the Chinese press were easier still. Although the assiduous and astute reader might have concluded that there was a danger of armed struggle, the MSS did not spell it out in their Journal.

The Journal did give considerable coverage to the fierce Malay reaction against the British attempt to bring the Malay States and Penang and Malacca together into a Union. It also reported at length on Indonesian subversive links, on the growth of Malay extremism, and the philosophy of the extremists in Indonesian-linked organisations such as the Angkatan Pemudaan who considered that independence must be won through struggle and bloodshed.

Malay and Indonesian subversion and the KMT, the Indian nationalists, and subversion of the trade unions and of the Chinese schools received the lion's share of coverage. In March 1947 there was a special six-page supplement on Chinese matters, but it was on the KMT not the MCP. In November the MCP rated less than one page in a twenty-seven-page issue. In December only two pages in a seventy-nine-page issue discussed the MCP.

On 15 January 1948 a translated secret MCP document was included but without analysis or comment on its significance. On 15 March there was a low-level report on an instruction from the Central Committee to Singapore: again without comment. One month later priorities were beginning to change and the MCP rated half a page. The Journal reported that the communists and their satellites were continuing with their activities. There were indications that communism was gaining ground, even among the Malayan peasantry, and evidence that the MCP were anticipating government action against them. Although the Journal noted that most of the leaders had gone underground, it did not relate this activity to preparation for armed struggle.

By the end of May the MSS had become better informed through captured documents and the interrogation of prisoners. It was the first significant hard intelligence about MCP activities to have appeared in the Journal since our agent Loi Tak's departure to Thailand in 1947. On 31 July the Journal gave the MCP pride of place with a twenty-one-page supplement. Much of the supplement was devoted to an MCP document describing the ramifications of the Loi Tak case. The MCP had lost track of him and had not expelled him from the MCP until December when they issued a detailed denunciation of their former Secretary General. The MSS went on to say that morale had been severely damaged by the Loi case. The MCP made a frantic plea to their members to trust their leaders and each other now that the case had been investigated and the culprit punished. The MSS concluded this issue of the Journal with reference to BMA arrests and banishments by remarking optimistically that measures should not be hampered by fear of world opinion and that all subversive organisations should be banned. Had they had more staff, and had their customers pressed for a focused threat assessment, their Political Journal would have been more likely to be enlightening.

Analysis of the pre-Emergency period and of the successes of the Emergency itself shows that poor intelligence structures and a lack of intelligence can both be remedied successfully.

2

VIETNAM

A CAN OF WORMS

'Dick, I need a paper on Viet Nam, and I'll tell you what I want included in it.'

President Johnson to Richard (Dick) Helms,
Director of Central Intelligence (DCI)

'CIA was the bearer of bad tidings throughout the Vietnam War, and [its analysis] was not very happily received by any of the policymakers'.

Ray Cline, Deputy Director of Central Intelligence (DDCI)

'We have been projecting an image of success over the recent months... Now, when we release the figure of 420,000–431,000, the newsmen will ... [draw] an erroneous and gloomy conclusion as to the meaning of the increase. ... In our view the strength figures for the SDF [Self Defence Forces] and SSDF [Secret Self Defence Forces] should be omitted entirely from the enemy strength figures.'

General Creighton Abrams, Deputy to General William Westmoreland,
US military commander, August 1967

The Vietnam War proffers a variety of lessons on intelligence. Better intelligence at the earlier stages of the might may have improved Western leaders' understanding of the nature of the problem posed by North Vietnam and their chances of success. An over-reliance on estimates of enemy numbers combined with limited understanding of the people of Vietnam led policymakers to make decisions that later proved questionable. Above all, there was a growing conflict between intelligence assessments and optimistic policymakers' opinions on the enemy's circumstances and the prospects of success. The Vietnam case is a prime example of a government indulging in wishful thinking for many years and ignoring inconvenient intelligence.

The observations about intelligence in the Vietnam War that follow are based on personal experience. I set out for Hanoi, the capital city of the Democratic Republic of Vietnam, the northern, communist half of Vietnam, in August 1967. I had been dragged away in a hurry from Kuala Lumpur without time to read up or meet experts. So my mind was open when I arrived in Hanoi. I was briefed by several officials in Saigon on my way, all of whom seemed to have swallowed General Westmoreland's line that the war of attrition was succeeding. My most useful meeting was with the Canadian Ambassador who invited me to look after the minute Canadian team in Hanoi, sheltering under the flag of the International Control Commission (ICC), which had been set up in order to monitor the ceasefire after the departure of the French in 1954. The ICC had long since ceased to be relevant but, unlike me, they had diplomatic privileges, and by some extraordinary stroke of luck their senior non-commissioned officer was, like me, a Black Watch veteran.

Driving into Hanoi we passed the Paul Doumer Bridge. A notice informed those who could read Chinese that the bridge had been repaired by the Chinese Army as a token of the eternal friendship between the people of China and Vietnam. The notice was a reminder that, for the moment, North Vietnam was receiving generous military support from China.

I had penetrated the bamboo curtain as the representative of a country which, although not actually engaged in the battlefield, was a close ally of the US. Saigon, the capital of South Vietnam, housed a large embassy, and was where Westmoreland and his staff were directing a vast military effort against the Vietnamese communists (known as the Vietcong, or the VC) in all its forms. It was not clear why the North Vietnamese allowed us to maintain our Hanoi post. Although we were not in any way belligerents, it was hardly a secret that we had some sympathy with the US. Perhaps the Vietnamese calculated that we could do little harm and might some day provide a useful link to Britain.

Twenty-five years later, however, they refused me a tourist visa, while the Chinese on the other hand never gave me the slightest problems when I returned as a private citizen.

For most of 1967 and 1968 I was based in Hanoi, where I was called Consul General by the British but Mr Stewart by the Vietnamese. The job was odd in that there were no British subjects in North Vietnam for me to look after, and there were not likely to be any so long as the war continued. It was a much more restricted post than Beijing and Shanghai. In Hanoi there were no British at all and there were few for-eigners apart from the diplomats and the ICC. The French were the only other Western diplomats in town. They, of course, were anti-American. My only friends were from the French, Indonesian, Egyptian and Indian contingents. The rest of the Diplomatic Corps were either from the Soviet Bloc or left-leaning Third World countries.

I am convinced that we more than earned our keep in this post, sup-plying a perspective on North Vietnam which was not available to our allies. It was a very privileged position to have: Western capitalist run-ning dogs of the American imperialists were not, in general, welcome. While there are considerable advantages to having an intelligence base housed in a diplomatic mission, the down side is that the enemy can usually identify the intelligence officers. There is no simple answer to whether this diplomatic cover solution is superior to the 'natural cover' solution. Establishing the latter is a slow process.

I did not have diplomatic privileges or immunity, a fact that made for serious reflection on the occasion that I was arrested by a mob of Red Guards and imprisoned. Our movements were severely restricted, so our choice of sources was small indeed. But we were on the ground, and so had a view denied to the embassies in Saigon. We could see the people and the shops, and draw some conclusions about the food situ-ation, health and morale. This direct experience was a valuable ingredi-ent for assessors struggling to put together an intelligence mosaic. I am sure that even if our assessment was gloomy, the US was grateful for our moral support.

I had little opportunity to discuss the war with officials. Except for brush contacts with members of the Politburo, the government's senior policymaking committee, at receptions, my only contact was with the Foreign Affairs Bureau of the Municipality. They were not anxious to develop a friendship. Nonetheless, the post gave me some feeling for the realities in North Vietnam, including a grandstand view of the air war in the sky above Hanoi. Having worked for so many years in Asia and learnt several Asian languages, I was in a better position to enjoy my posting than most foreign diplomats. It was not difficult for me to learn the basics of Vietnamese and read my way round the town while my colleagues remained 'blind'. My reports from Hanoi, which can be read in The National Archives in London, are a reminder of how much one can learn without secret sources, a lesson that was reinforced during my time in China (see Chapter Three).

My experience working in Asia helped me to avoid mirror imaging, the label often given to the trap of assuming that everyone thinks the way that you do (see Chapter Six). It was understandable that the army of Westerners and analysts, knowing the conditions in which the North Vietnamese regular and irregular forces lived, and the weight of bombs thrown against their country, should conclude that morale must be low and the Politburo ready to negotiate; and no doubt anti-communist sources in the South anxious to encourage the US to continue the fight exaggerated the plight of the North Vietnamese. But my hunches were proved right when the North Vietnamese fought on until the US became tired. It mattered little whether the enemy numbered 300,000 (the military's estimate) or 600,000 (the CIA's estimate, which took into account irregular forces). What mattered more than their numbers were morale and the determination of the communist leaders.

Historical Background and Overview of the War

The territory now known as Vietnam had, for two thousand years, suffered foreign invasions, shifting frontiers and cultural intrusions. By the middle of the nineteenth century the French were moving from a missionary presence to the development of a colonial government. The seeds of the Vietnam War were sown during the Second World War. The Japanese, constrained by their membership of the Tripartite Axis (Germany, Italy and Japan) dealt softly with the Vichy French and the Vietnamese, so the VC (the communists) did not suffer, as the MCP had, from the attentions of the Japanese Secret Police.

In March 1945 the Japanese took off the velvet gloves, deposed the French and installed Bao Dai as puppet Emperor. The Free French had not yet arrived, and so an unfortunate British general, Douglas Gracey, had, from August 1945, the thankless task of trying to keep order in the mess as communists and criminals stepped into the vacuum. When the French Army arrived they found themselves facing a belligerent and increasingly powerfully armed Communist Party leading a United Front, which demanded that the French relinquish their colonial claims. Having mounted a guerrilla war Ho Chi Minh, the leader of the VC, declared himself President of Vietnam. In December 1945 the first French naval shell was fired at Hanoi. The new war had started.

It was in 1954, after a catastrophic defeat, that the French gave up their supposedly impregnable fortress at Dien Bien Phu, built to show the VC that the French could dominate the hinterland. They had planned to supply, reinforce and support the fortress by air, but General Vo Nguyen Giap managed to drag the VC's guns up the steep hills overlooking Dien Bien Phu and so interdicted their logistics. The defeat was a demonstration that a 'raggedy-assed, little fourth-rate country' (the phrase used ten years later by President Johnson) might be able, with ingenuity coupled to muscle power and fighting spirit, to defeat a more powerful opponent. It was, of course, ironic that the US, traditionally deep-rooted critics of all forms of colonialism, should pick up the baton, and they were woefully unprepared for the mammoth and complex nature of the long-term postcolonial task ahead.

The US' Decades of Intervention

The 1954 Geneva Agreement divided Vietnam along the 17th Parallel into a communist North and a non-communist South. As the French withdrew the US began to increase their presence, and soon the US was contributing 75 per cent of the South Vietnam Government budget. By 1963 the US Military Advisory Group numbered nearly 17,000, but many of the South Vietnam Army (ARVN) made poor use of US weapons and training. The Vietnamese leaders failed throughout the war to convince the young people of South Vietnam that the anti-communist cause was worth dying for. The hearts and minds campaign, which had been central to success in Malaya by persuading the people to support the British rather than the CTs, could not be replicated in Vietnam.

In August 1964 a report alleging that a North Vietnamese torpedo boat had attacked the US Destroyer Maddox in the Gulf of Tonkin gave Johnson a pretext for a dramatic increase in US military involvement.

By 1965 there were 81,400 US soldiers on the ground. By 1973, when the US withdrew, there were over half a million and Westmoreland was claiming that a further 100,000 would do the job.

Of course US military officers believed that the VC could not continue the battle in the face of massive aerial bombardment of their industries and their infrastructure. It was difficult for regular officers serving in the most sophisticated and logistically well endowed army in the world to grasp the strength of a peasant army. The needs of the North Vietnamese Army (NVA) could be met by gangs of 'coolies' pushing bicycles which might carry as much as 200 kilograms of supplies. Their supply route, the Ho Chi Minh Trail, could not be destroyed by aerial bombardment; the Commander in Chief, Pacific Command (CINCPAC) once showed me aerial photographs with fresh tracks making a detour round every crater, so that within hours of a successful bombardment the bicycle convoy could once more trickle southwards.

A senior US State Department official remarked to me that, since the US did not have any equivalent to our Colonial Service to provide officers ready to immerse themselves for the long-term in Vietnamese culture and language, the battle was probably hopeless. Officers, temporarily seconded from the State Department, the CIA and the police and so on, however energetic, could not be expected to perform as effectively as Colonial Service Officers who had chosen to specialise overseas. The US soon discovered, as they did in Afghanistan and Iraq after the terrorist attacks of 11 September 2001 (9/11), that it was easier to win battles than to win hearts and minds or to help a foreign country where there was no effective administration. Not that winning battles is any easier, especially when the public at home turns against a war because of the number of soldiers returning in body bags.

Robert McNamara, Secretary of Defence from 1961 to 1968, and the business-trained people, whom he had introduced into the Pentagon, were led astray by the pseudo science of the numbers game, a danger that all would do well to be wary of. Their extrapolations from numbers, such as enemy body counts and the weight of bombs dropped, supported an assessment that the enemy was bleeding to death. Their assessments of the effects of bombing the Ho Chi Minh Trail ignored the difference between the heavy logistical requirements of a Western army and the light requirements of VC foot soldiers, and the fact that, since the VC armaments came from Soviet and Chinese factories, the bombing of North Vietnam had no effect on armament production. As the war dragged on, McNamara became increasingly uneasy, yet his official assessments for the President still continued to be optimistic.

A newly retired US general told me that he had left the army because he could see no merit in the war and that when he had polled almost 200 retired generals, to his astonishment the majority had expressed doubts about the US objective. The same general described to me the numbers game as it was played in Saigon. The staff were required to compile reports on military progress which was based on over sixty so-called statistical indicators, such as the numbers of enemy and kill ratios. This methodology produced a stream of optimistic reports leading to the conclusion that the North Vietnamese would be unable to continue the fight. But my general remarked, 'unfortunately in this war the will power as well as material power was required.' It was true that the US had the power but the Vietcong had the will.

Not all presidential advisers were optimistic. As early as 1961, John Kenneth Galbraith, the US's Ambassador to India, the country which chaired the ICC, wrote a report for President John F. Kennedy in which he said '[Ngo Dinh] Diem [the President of South Vietnam] will not reform either administratively or politically in any effective way' and that Diem had 'effectively resisted improvement for a long while in [the] face of heavy deterioration.' In December 1962 Senator Mike Mansfield told the Senate that despite the US's two billion dollar investment, 'after seven years of the Republic, South Vietnam appears less, not more stable'. By 1963 Kennedy had begun to consider disengagement.

An early State Department assessment predicted that President Diem would fall, 500,000 US troops would be sucked into the conflict and the war would last for at least ten years. The authors of such gloomy reports were endangering their careers: such pessimistic appreciations are easily dismissed as defeatist. Unpalatable assessments also came from elsewhere. In 1966, for example, a group of forty-seven non-government specialists were brought together by the Institute of Defence Analysis to look at the results of twelve months of 'Rolling Thunder', the heavy air bombardment of the North. The group, which had access to all intelligence which was available to the US Government, concluded that the bombing had not affected North Vietnam's will to fight, nor created serious difficulties in transportation, economy or morale.

McNamara eventually lost confidence in his number-based methodology. In his 1995 autobiography he confessed:[1]

'We misjudged ... the geopolitical intentions of our adversaries...'

This may be true but not of central importance.

'We viewed the people and leaders of South Vietnam in terms of our own experience. We saw in them a thirst for—and a determination to fight for—freedom and democracy. We totally misjudged the political forces within the country.'

The naiveté in seeing a thirst for democracy is an example of mirror imaging. There was indeed a misjudgement of the political forces.

'We underestimated the power of nationalism to motivate a people ... to fight and die for their beliefs and values ...'

This comment suggests insufficient expertise on patriotism. McNamara might have added 'and the strength of resentment against foreign occupation'.

'Our misjudgements of friend and foe alike reflected our profound ignorance of the history, culture, and politics of the people in the area, and the personalities and habits of their leaders.'

This is spot on: the ignorance was profound.

'We failed ... to recognize the limitations of modern, high-technology military equipment, forces, and doctrine, in confronting unconventional, highly-motivated people's movements.'

This was a further example of the US having fallen into the trap of mirror imaging.

'We failed to recognize that in international affairs ... there may be problems for which there are no immediate solutions.'

A depressing but sensible realisation. This failure was an example of wishful thinking: mixing hope with reality.

'[We failed] to organize the top echelons of the executive branch [in the US] to deal effectively with the extraordinarily complex range of political and military issues [in Vietnam].'

A not unusual failure to educate the end user of intelligence.

This is a refreshing litany of self-criticism by a Cabinet Officer who had held major policy responsibility for the conduct of the war. It confirmed the comments I had made in my final despatches from Hanoi in

1968. My last one noted that there was no sign of a break in the will of the party or the spirit of the people, which might have justified hope of significant concessions to bring the bombing to an end or to achieve an early peace. It continued by noting that the withdrawal of foreign troops remained at the top of the agenda at peace talks. The intentions of the Politburo as seen from Hanoi gave little reason for optimism, and the best hope for peace seemed to be that if the US strengthened the ARVN and started to withdraw its troops, the communists would allow the war to simmer down. This fade out seemed to be the only immediate alternative to a continuation of the war.

It was daunting to remember that my one man band was competing with an army of analysts in Saigon, but on the face of it I was right and they were wrong. It was difficult for Western assessors to grasp that although all the indicators in use in Saigon suggested that the Vietcong were losing, this did not mean that morale was cracking. The Hanoi population were on short commons, the city was shabby and life austere, but morale held firm, despite the bombings. Morale was more important than military power in Vietnam, where the Vietcong were fighting on home ground and the invaders were thousands of miles from home and had difficulty in understanding why they were there.

The intelligence personnel preparing figures purporting to show the strength of the NVA made decisions that had the undesirable effect of misleading the recipients of this intelligence. US military estimates omitted militia, guerrillas and civilian irregulars from the total strength of the NVA. This military definition, in effect only considering uniformed soldiers, produced a strength of about 300,000, while the inclusion of the non-uniformed supporters produced a figure of 600,000. A compromise was reached whereby no numbers were given for the non-uniformed irregulars and this manipulation of figures gave false encouragement to the US Government. The Tet Offensive revealed that this optimism was misplaced.

The Tet Offensive

In January 1968, Westmoreland reported that the previous year 'ended with the enemy increasingly resorting to desperation [sic] tactics... The friendly picture gives rise to optimism for increased successes in 1968.' By 25 January intelligence led him to report instead that events seem to be 'shaping up as a D-Day for widespread pre-Tet offensive action on the part of VC/NVA forces.'

The Tet (Spring Festival) Offensive of 31 January 1968 marked the beginning of the end of the US intervention. The VC launched a countrywide assault, penetrated into the heart of Saigon, captured Hue, the ancient capital of Annam, and occupied many towns. Westmoreland boasted that the offensive had been defeated, while Hanoi boasted that they had punched formidable holes. Both proclaimed a famous victory. But Johnson was faced with an increasingly hostile media and population who asked how, if previous assertions that the US were winning were correct, the VC's offensive had been so successful. Hanoi had demonstrated that they could still give an excellent account of themselves in a fire fight, and Hanoi's declaration of a great victory would not be challenged in the Hanoi media.

Soon after the Tet Offensive I was invited to Singapore where our Ambassador in Saigon and I were to lead a discussion. The participants would be senior men from the diplomatic, military and intelligence professions. As I flew south for the conference, the more I thought about the debate and the more worried I became. I was outgunned: it was to be a Consul General against a senior Ambassador, and one against many, all of whom had access to intelligence and appreciations from the US juggernaut in Saigon and knew better than to challenge Westmoreland's view. I decided, therefore, not to waste my breath but to write a document entitled 'Notional Appreciation of the Tet Offensive by the Hanoi Politburo' and to ask the meeting to read it. As I had anticipated there was no support for my gloomy analysis that, while it was true that the communists had not achieved their final objective, they had done huge damage to South Vietnamese morale and won a propaganda victory.

Personal Reflections

Bias, complacency and over-reliance on technology all played their part in the failure in Vietnam, but ignorance of history also made a major contribution. A nation that had beaten the British Regular Army in the eighteenth century should have been better able to understand the strength of an irregular force fighting on home ground against a regular army from abroad.

Throughout my time in Hanoi I reported that morale remained high among the Vietnamese. They were determined to fight on until, like the Chinese long before and the French more recently, the US decided to go home. After Hanoi, I met some of the principal US players in this war: Dick Helms, DCI, William (Bill) Colby, a future DCI, and others. I found that my views were in most respects shared by the CIA's intelligence wing.

On my way back to Britain I called on Helms, the DCI of the day. He was pessimistic. He saw the growing anti-war feeling all round, not merely among students and parents, and assumed correctly that soon the US would have to seek a way out of a war which had already taken the lives of 15,000 US soldiers. I found it uncomfortable to be mixing with friends in the operations and intelligence side of the CIA whose daily work was to support the war effort in Vietnam when they did not believe in the war or that it could be won. Many of them were troubled because their children were about to be drafted, or were being sucked into the peace movement. I also once had the opportunity to debate these topics with Zbigniew Brzezinski the Presidential Adviser. He agreed that the US had underestimated the will of the North Vietnamese.

Yet there were still civilians who were confident of victory in the long-term. Among them was an old friend, Bill Colby, a devout Roman Catholic and a committed anti-communist, who later became Director of the CIA. In my Hanoi time Colby was Director of the Pacification programme, which had borrowed heavily from Malayan experience. He remained certain that had the US persevered the communists would give up the armed struggle. He did not take into account the limited appetite of US society for a long painful war on the other side of the world nor that in Malaya we had been part of the government, not merely advisers.

The US should, however, be given credit for its role in preventing the fall of other non-communist dominoes in South East Asia. Some argue that the domino theory was disproved by the fact that, although the VC won in Vietnam, the rest of the dominoes in South East Asia did not fall. But without the US's intervention the outcome might have been very different. The twenty years that intervened between the withdrawal of the French and the withdrawal of the US gave a breathing space to the potential dominoes of Malaysia, Singapore, Thailand and Indonesia.

The Intelligence Performance

The Vietnam War has been scrutinised in a multitude of public and private inquires; most in the spirit of a search for scapegoats in the tradition of the investigations that responded to the Pearl Harbor disaster. The evidence suggests that overall the intelligence community did a good job, although they were never able to satisfy their customers, nor able to provide a clear warning that Giap might be about to break the Tet truce and launch an attack on Saigon, Hue and other towns.

The CIA's Intelligence Directorate was not guilty of over-optimism. A CIA paper dated 2 December 1967 said that there was no evidence of a weakening of the communist will. Although US intelligence recognised Giap's tactical skills because of his resounding victory at Dien Bien Phu, it underestimated his talent as a strategist and as a consequence intelligence did not look for a strategic plan. The ferocity of the attack on the US's Khe San base in January 1968 convinced US intelligence that the NVA intended to inflict a crippling defeat on US forces in the tradition of Dien Ben Phu. The Khe San operation was a brilliant deception ploy that seemed to provide good evidence that Giap was engaging in a battle for the countryside.

Insufficient weight was given to intelligence from the ARVN. So when, immediately before the Tet Offensive captured VC tapes suggested that the VC were taking an unhealthy interest in the cities, the reports were not highlighted. Intelligence professionals believed the stories that Giap had disappeared from public view because he had fallen out of political favour. This was wishful thinking: instead, he was busy planning the Tet Offensive.

Intelligence reporting was insufficiently wary of the optimistic reports about the strength of anti-communist feeling in South Vietnam. There seemed to be little awareness of the danger that informants might have a motive to provide information designed to please their US contacts and to encourage them to continue the battle. Reports that contradicted the rosy picture of ardent anti-communists were likely to get short shrift. And intelligence did not emphasise the fact that, although people may have been anti-communist, they did not enjoy a host of trigger-happy foreign troops swarming over their country. If McNamara's team had been augmented by people who had studied the intelligence lessons of the past, he might have learned much earlier how flawed his assessment system was. On the other hand, perhaps such a person, rocking boats by challenging mirror imaging and commonly held opinions, could not have worked in the Pentagon. Ultimately the outcome of the war depended on the workings of the human mind: endurance, morale, loyalty, national pride, and so on. You can count the number of tanks, discover their technical specifications, capabilities, and reliability, but you can only guess about human spirit and willpower as the Germans found to their cost at the battle of Stalingrad in 1942–3.

The Malayan Red Herring

Whether the conflicts are examined in terms of intelligence lessons alone, or lessons to be drawn from other aspects, differences abound between the Malayan Emergency and the Vietnam War. The fundamental reason why there was little chance of replicating the Malayan victory in Vietnam, however, was that in Malaya we had been part of the government, whereas in Vietnam the US was not and the governments they were trying to support were ineffective.

I did not expect that the musings of an ex-Malayan civil servant temporarily living in Hanoi would have much impact. Westmoreland, unlike Templer in Malaya, could not grasp the fact that the solution depended as much on politics as on military might. Furthermore, I doubted that the advice of my old ex-Malayan friends in the British Advisory Group in Saigon could be of much help. It was true that the enemy in both cases were communists, and that both countries were in South East Asia, but there the similarities ended.

Militarily the differences could hardly have been greater. The VC was receiving generous aid from the Soviet Union and China; men for their anti-aircraft defences, training teams, engineers to repair their roads and bridges. By contrast, the only support the MCP got from their communist brothers was rhetoric. Most of the MCP soldiers, never more than 12,000 strong, had been skulking in jungle camps, surrendered or retired to sanctuary in Thailand. The VC armed forces, numbering hundreds of thousands were fighting major battles, controlled more than half the country and had railways, ports and airfields.

In Malaya we were a colonial government and were working, not as dictators, but as co-leaders of a multi-racial team. We spoke Malay, Chinese and Indian languages, earned respect by studying the local customs and spent a lot of time with the local people. Unlike the French in

Vietnam who exercised direct rule, we ruled indirectly through local people. Each Malay State had a Malay ruler, and the British were 'Advisers'.

And then there was the carrot of independence. Our intention to leave Malaya in 1957 had been well publicised, so MCP rhetoric about the need to fight to gain independence had no resonance. No such agreement had been made between the French and the Vietnamese; President Charles de Gaulle's talk of 'autonomy proportionate to her progress and attainments', was hardly the sort of offer to assuage the thirst of an ardent patriot like Ho Chi Minh.

The composition of the two national Communist Parties was also very different. In Vietnam the Party was led by a national hero, Ho Chi Minh, whose liberation credentials went back to 1920 when, as Nguyen Ai Quoc (Nguyen, lover of his country), he had spoken out vehemently in Paris, contrasting the French motto *Liberte Egalite Fraternite* with the reality of the French behaviour in Indo China. In Malaya, on the other hand, Secretary General Chin Peng, who had replaced Loi Tak, was almost unknown. Most members of the MCP were Chinese and so they had no nationalist credentials, whereas most members of the Vietnamese Communist Party were of Indochinese stock.

This short analysis suggests that our Malayan experience was of limited relevance to the US in Vietnam. This is a reminder of the limitations of attempting to transfer lessons directly from one conflict to another. I am still looking for a satisfactory explanation for the MCP's touching faith that the people of Malaya would rise up to support them. Chin Peng's 2003 autobiographical work does not provide an answer.[2] Sir Robert Thompson's (formerly Secretary for Defence in Malaya) advisory team to Vietnam was of limited help in a situation that was so totally different. In the absence of viable, dynamic, political leadership able to rally the population against the VC, the Malayan precedent was almost irrelevant. The essential political foundations for victory, which Templer emphasised in Malaya, were lacking in Vietnam.

Among the lessons learnt by Western policymakers from the Vietnam War was to be wary of engaging in asymmetrical warfare against a country vastly smaller and vastly outgunned but no less determined to fight for independence. Intelligence is only one ingredient in success: there may be factors in the enemy's favour that are difficult to eliminate, such as morale and assistance from third party sources. What intelligence can help with is the identification of a 'best practice' approach whilst measuring the chances of success. The Vietnam case clearly shows the danger of the numbers game and mirror imaging, and how these two fallacies can exacerbate one another.

3

CHINESE AFFAIRS

'The enlightened sovereign and the capable commander ... achieve successes far surpassing those of ordinary people because they possess "foreknowledge". This "foreknowledge" cannot be obtained from ghosts or spirits, nor from gods, nor by analogy with past events, nor from astrological calculations. It can only come from men who know the enemy situation.'

Sun Tzu, 'The Art of War', fifth century BC

'He who lacks wisdom cannot use agents.'

Sun Tzu, 'The Art of War', fifth century BC

'He who makes full assessment of the situation at the pre-war council meeting ... is more likely to win.'

Sun Tzu, 'The Art of War', fifth century BC

This chapter looks at China through my eyes over a period of almost sixty years working in the Colonial Service, Foreign Office and finally as a business adviser. During those years I worked with many Chinese colleagues in the diaspora as well as in mainland China, watching the country throw off the shackles of ideology and develop into a world economic power. The experiences related by this chapter illustrate how much can be done with eyes and ears and friendships without indulging in clandestine intelligence activities. The degree of control that totalitarian states have over the amount and type of open source material available does not prevent the collection of overt intelligence, as the example of journalistic material demonstrates. Creativity and skill can prove productive when seeking intelligence in such states. Indeed, these are useful when engaging in the art of intelligence no matter what the target.

My interest in China began in 1946 when I became a Cadet in the Malayan Civil Service and was sent to learn Chinese in Singapore and in China. By the time that I returned to Malaya the civil war known officially as the 'Emergency' was in full swing; the MCP, whose members were mainly Malayan Chinese, had gone to war. So the Chinese-speaking members of the Malayan Civil Service—the Chinese Affairs personnel—found themselves at the centre of the action.

In a country as large as China the general public can be as ignorant as the foreigners. In 1948 few Chinese knew what hell Yenan, Mao Tsetung's base in North West China, had been. Yenan was little more than a vast gulag, where speech and thought were censored and communication with the outside world was forbidden. Foreign ignorance of the truth was understandable: Edgar Snow was the only Western writer in Yenan and he chose not to describe the misery. He earned his reputation by reporting Yenan as some sort of a communist paradise.

I returned to China in 1960, joining the British Diplomatic Mission in Beijing and, the following year, becoming the Consul General Shanghai. My years in Beijing and Shanghai coincided with a lull between the miseries that came with Mao's Great Leap Forward and the Cultural Revolution. Mao had shown his true nature and China was reeling from a series of brutal campaigns designed to revolutionise the country regardless of the pain and misery caused. Mao set young against old, children against parents, students against teachers, workers against management, coining idiotic slogans such as 'better red than expert', disparaging all traditional learning and art, and mocking antiquities. He demonstrated that he was not interested in the welfare of the Chinese. But we Westerners did not appreciate the depth of misery and starvation which had been brought about by ambitious policies. We were not allowed to see the famine and poverty in the countryside. We could guess that the leaves of the trees around Beijing had disappeared into the locals' cooking pots, but we did not know that throughout the country-side millions were starving to death. Fellow travelling foreign journalists concealed the truth, and any brave Chinese leaders who challenged Mao were dismissed.

Sometimes one was able to help the search for truth. I made a contribution when, in the early 1960s, my Head of Mission, the UK's most senior representative in China, asked for confirmation of the rumour that there had been a serious breakdown in Sino-Soviet relations and that the 12,000 Russian experts and their wives were being sent home. My response was to immediately monitor the railway station. While the rest of the diplomatic community were still debating the rumour we observed thousands of Russian experts and their loot-laden wives boarding the trains to Moscow. The Sino-Soviet relationship was indeed in trouble. The Sovietologists, the intelligence community and academia's specialists on the Soviet Union, were prone to take inexplicable Soviet stories as disinformation, and were no doubt surprised to find that this time the rumour was true.

The Chinese Security authorities must have gnashed their teeth over the fact that foreigners were able, from bases outside China, to intercept the Chinese internal public broadcasts. Local newspapers also provided some information. The bar at the top of Beijing's Qianmen Hotel was of help too. This was the drinking hole of the few journalists who had somehow managed to obtain a visa. The visitors in my time included Han Su Yin. I did not tell her that I had been responsible for banning her book about Malaya. Of course, all these people were 'fellow travellers'. They earned their visas by reporting that China was in good shape, and by repeating the statements of the senior Chinese they interviewed. However, Su Yin was half Chinese and the West found it easy to believe the rosy picture she painted. She was badly caught out later, however, when the Cultural Revolution ended and the horrific truth emerged.

On several occasions I had to use my Chinese language skills to extricate foreign Ambassadors who had been taking photographs. Usually the problem was some peasant soldier or police officer who had been brainwashed into believing that all foreigners were spies; sometimes it was an overzealous local who thought that a picturesque dilapidated temple was not an appropriate subject for a picture. On one occasion the head of the British Foreign Office was arrested in the Western Hills when looking for the temple where he had lived as a young language student. I knew that we were slightly out of bounds but I was able to extricate our distinguished visitor by warning the Chinese soldiers, who surrounded us with bayonets fixed, that they would be responsible if they prevented our party from attending the banquet to which their

Foreign Minister had invited us. Fortunately I had a cutting from a Beijing newspaper supporting my tale. I often rescued Ambassadors who were guilty of nothing more sinister than their incompetence with their expensive cameras and thus lingered too long in one place.

The Chinese authorities tolerated my non-diplomatic habits although the Shanghai Public Security Bureau (PSB) warned my best Chinese friend that she should not be seeing me because I was too 'sharp'. Fortunately she paid no attention. However the PSB did their best to discourage me from travelling by delaying my permits until the last moment assuming I would have no time to buy tickets. They had not recognised that I spoke Chinese and was quite capable of buying tickets at the railway station by myself. I made the most of these chances to see more of China.

But what, you may ask, was the benefit to Her Majesty's Government of all this travel? It was true that I was not collecting any information that in a democratic open society could be called secret. But we were in a police state and foreigners were only supposed to know the Party line. In the two cities where foreigners lived, court notices, legal information, sentencing and so on were not displayed. By contrast, the smaller cities seldom visited by foreigners were festooned with interesting notices, and the PSB forgot that some of us could read Chinese.

These public notices provided a commentary on the scene which was not to be found in the national papers. Small beer indeed, but beer denied to those who never left the capital, and could not read Chinese. To a limited extent I could do the job of a military attaché, using eyes and ears. I had an advantage over the rest of the embassy staff; I had spent a great deal more time in Chinese society than they.

My use of these kinds of intelligence sources allowed me to predict that Deng Xiaoping would become the leader of China, but not that he would open China to the world. Fortunately my Ambassador seemed to approve of my methods. I became his tourist guide, and the papers in The National Archives suggest that London and Washington appreciated my reporting, which was based on open source material. Yet no-one understood Mao. We could only guess that there were dissident voices in his councils. I had pleaded with Nien Cheng, my friend in Shanghai, that she should stay away when she next made one of her regular business trips to Hong Kong before there was another campaign against bourgeois Chinese with Western connections. But it did not occur to either of us that the next campaign would be much more violent: that Mao would rather wreck China than give power to moderates. Three years later the Cultural Revolution followed. I missed it but Nien spent five years in solitary confinement accused, among other things, of espionage.[1]

Nien was certainly not an agent. Her background knowledge of the China scene was, however, invaluable to me. When, for example, the Embassies in Beijing were worrying about the appearance of masses of Chinese pressing against the border fence around Hong Kong, wondering whether China was about to swamp the area, Nien correctly assessed that this was an accident. The Canton Authorities had relaxed their exit rules and the public was simply trying to emigrate. We failed to understand the scale of the disasters created by Mao's policies and no-one, Chinese or foreign, foresaw the Cultural Revolution.

My diplomatic spell in China had coincided with the winding down of the Great Leap Forward that had installed a steel plant in every village, communal feeding, and interference in agricultural practices. I was lucky to leave before the Cultural Revolution. My successor stood in the sun for a day in Shanghai confronted by baying mobs, and our embassy in Beijing was invaded and burnt. Foreign observers did not know the scale of the disasters nor the depth of the tensions between Mao and his senior colleagues. Those who strongly opposed policies which starved China in order to allow Mao to play the rich uncle to the Third World were hounded to painful deaths.

In 1982 I returned to China as an adviser to companies anxious to exploit the 'opening' of the PRC. When Deng Xiaoping became leader of China in 1978 he began to lead the country into a new relationship with the world, one in which it began to open its doors to cooperation and to seek investment. It took many years to undo the collectivist ideas which for thirty years had plagued modern China, but by 1980 a start had been made by encouraging small businesses. It was remarkable how much I was able to achieve without institutional support. I met Jiang Zemin at a time that the China-watching community had never heard of him, shortly before he became President of China, and proceeded with his help and that of his Chief Scientist to find a great deal of useful, profitable business.

As for predictions, I did rather better than most of the pundits who in the 1980s, year after year, warned that China was heading for a crash. Their judgement, I think, was coloured by irritation that China was not listening to our talk about human rights, democracy and rule of law. Thirty years later China still seems to be doing quite well.

All of these tales from China are illustrations of how much can be achieved without secret sources. Long service in Asia, making friends and using my eyes and ears was the basis for my activities, not spying. It is rare for diplomats, reporters, academics or intelligence officers to be allowed to specialise as I did. There were reporters like Dennis Bloodworth who stuck with Asia but they were rare birds indeed.

Here we might come back to a central problem about assessment. Analysts are easily and constantly influenced by the priorities of their own cultures. They find it hard to remember that other countries have different priorities. It was I suppose easier for me, having so many Chinese friends over so many years, to remember. For two happy years in the 1940s I immersed myself in Chinese life assisted by five teachers who were as much friends as tutors. Three were men dressed in scholars' gowns: a seventy-year old roué, Him Po, smoking opium and a mine of information on Chinese society; his brother, Ah Baat, married to a millionaire's daughter; the third a son of the last Manchu commander in Canton. Twenty years later, in Beijing, at 6 a.m. every morning I continued my language and cultural studies, struggling through the daily papers with my teachers' help, improving my Mandarin and learning the communist jargon. My colleagues and I assumed that all our Chinese contacts were subject to PSB control and monitoring and acted accordingly. Nevertheless these daily conversations helped me to assess information through the lens of locals. It remains a mystery why the authorities sent me such delightful unreconstructed teachers.

Conclusion

The insight that I had gained during my student days and official postings to China proved very useful when I returned as a business adviser. It soon became apparent that I was 'one up' on the other foreign companies trying to break into the China market, who were all flying blind, advised by hosts of bankers, lawyers and consultants. Knowing the Chinese language I was on the inside track. Twenty-five years later I left a retired Chinese Major General of Signals to take my place. A career in intelligence is not necessarily a handicap to a further career.

PART TWO

THE MACHINERY AND METHODOLOGY
OF INTELLIGENCE

4

THE ORGANISATION AND MACHINERY
OF INTELLIGENCE

'There is no room for either politics or partisanship in the way the intelligence community performs its functions.'

George Tenet, DCI, 2001

'I want one dog to kick, but when it comes to intelligence, I have to go down to the pound!'

Donald Rumsfeld, Secretary of Defence

'[P]ut good people in those jobs, give them clear direction and hold them accountable for their performance, and I think that's probably more important than whatever reporting arrangements we have.'

Richard Cheney, Vice President to George W. Bush, 2002

This chapter, discussing the machinery of an intelligence community, reminds us that failure may occur at any stage of the intelligence process; so there is little point in talking of intelligence failure without pinpointing which part or parts of the machine failed. The complexity of the machinery of intelligence and security in modern times, whether in a democratic or a police state, is immense, and we can only scratch the surface of the topic here. The electronic revolution has brought new techniques of intelligence collection and therefore innumerable new opportunities and problems for security and intelligence agencies, which need an ever-growing army of people for mundane tasks such as record keeping and tracing. The computer enables such matters as cross references to be dealt with at a speed well beyond the capacity of what the CIA used to affectionately call 'the ladies in tennis shoes': but unlike those ladies the computer has no folk memory. In the 1970s, the CIA's operational officers were already bemoaning the retirement of their ladies with their card indexes and elephantine memories; they cannot be entirely replicated by computers. The human element at all levels and in all forms of activity, remains an essential factor.

Computers and computer systems can be magical, powerful tools, but they also bring problems with them. Edward Snowden's leaks of classified material have reminded the US Government of these potential problems. Kim Philby and his contemporary spies had to handle reams of paper. The size and weight of paper involved in an operational plan in earlier days would probably have reminded even the dizziest of staff officers of the importance of the package they were carrying. Computers can be crammed full with highly sensitive material, and occasionally some officer who should know better leaves their laptop lying around.

There is a further danger in the reliance on computers, which may not be recognised: in pre-laptop days a case officer could rely on a secretary to follow through on the paperwork while the case officer continued their operational duties. Since a case officer's reputation is more likely to be built on success as an agent recruiter and a producer of intelligence than on the perfection of their records, it is doubtful whether all are as meticulous today as secretaries used to be about record keeping.

The simplest way to consider the intelligence process is as a chain linking the customers—those who receive intelligence from the intelligence services—through assessment, to the material that is reported by the collectors of intelligence. A simplified 'intelligence chain' is set out below:

1. The customers (political and military decision makers).
2. The final judgement of the intelligence community (in Britain this is produced by the JIC).
3. The assessors (in Britain, since 1968, this work has been done in the Cabinet Office).
4. The analysts (Defence Intelligence, scientists, and specialists).

5. Collectors and sources. In Britain these are:
   a) MI5 (security intelligence).
   b) SIS (foreign intelligence, based in the UK but operating around the world).
   c) An independent signals intelligence agency (GCHQ).
   d) Other official sources (military and diplomatic).
   e) Open sources of every kind (media, academic, social).

Each stage should contribute to a solidly based opinion ready to present to the customer. Of course, the theory is easier than the practice. The collector may have difficulty in validating a sub source. The analysts and assessors may subconsciously give the benefit of the doubt to material that supports the received wisdom. Intelligence might be passed on to the consumer in its raw form, because of time pressures, leaving it liable to criticism or even refutation at a later date. In addition, there is nothing to stop a strong willed Prime Minister from insisting on seeing the raw material as Churchill did. But national leaders, who insist on being their own Intelligence Chiefs, can do great harm to their nations and the world. The machinery discussed in this chapter is the ideal, but even in a democratic government inconvenient intelligence can be rejected or ignored. This chapter concerns the parts of the intelligence community, including comment on the US example that I have observed, the British example, which I have participated in, and the roles that customers, assessors, analysts and collectors of intelligence should play in trying to produce national intelligence answers.

Coordination of an Intelligence Community

'I am going to force them [the intelligence bureaucracies] to cooperate.'

John M. (Mike) McConnell, Director of National Intelligence (DNI), 2007

'The objective should be that processing of deployment orders and obtaining other bureaucratic clearances can be accomplished in minutes and hours, not days and weeks.'

Donald Rumsfeld, Secretary of Defence, 2002

Coordination is a fine concept, but effective coordination is hard to achieve. Coordinating so complex a machine, employing an army of people, is a monumentally difficult problem. Obviously there should be an attempt to coordinate, but we should be realistic about expectations. In 1968 Sir Dick White, formerly Head first of MI5 and then of SIS, was appointed to the newly created Cabinet post of Intelligence Coordinator; but he knew full well the limitations of his role. The intelligence and security agencies were independent organisations with their own budgets, and they were not subordinate to the Coordinator, or even to the JIC. Their masters were elsewhere in Whitehall: the Foreign Office, Home Office, and Ministry of Defence. White was an adviser: the only thing he commanded was respect. If the intelligence agencies or the JIC did not like his advice, they were at liberty to ignore it.

The US experience

The US intelligence community faces the largest problem of national coordination in the Western world. It has a growing annual budget well over $50 billion and employs over 100,000 people. Even if all were part of a uniformed, disciplined service, their efforts would be hard to coordinate. But most are civilians from a variety of disciplines and backgrounds. It took the US fifty years from the creation of their first civilian intelligence agency, the CIA, to recognise the folly of expecting one person to be simultaneously both director of the CIA and director of the national intelligence community. The popular title of intelligence Tsar is bandied about, but it is easier to stop people doing things, than to coordinate and to inspire people to drop petty jealousies.

Soldiers at war are motivated to help their comrades in defence or attack, but there is no civilian equivalent to that camaraderie. The term intelligence community, with its connotations of shared values and collegiate spirit, is misleading. This is a community where, in the US for example, as Director of the Federal Bureau of Investigation (FBI), J. Edgar Hoover once ordered his staff not to speak to CIA officers. The term intelligence circus is, perhaps, more appropriate. The tent is large, the individual performers often brilliant, but the lion tamer has a very different persona to the acrobat or the clown. Similarly the spymaster is likely to have a totally different persona to a research officer, cryptographer or scientist. The only certain common factor in the intelligence circus is that everyone in the community is on the government payroll; but that does not guarantee collegiality.

The US's Intelligence Reform and Terrorism Prevention Act of 2004 created the post of Director of National Intelligence. The post-holder has the coordinating role previously assigned to the DCI, and has authority over the community's budgets. Within two years, though, the first DNI, John Negroponte, moved on to the less complex subject of diplomacy. His successor, Mike McConnell, a retired four-star Admiral of the US Navy, with excellent credentials as a former Director of the National Security Agency (NSA), soon discovered that the problems he faced were greater than any he had faced in the US Navy. The CIA used to say that it was difficult to identify the main enemy; at times the enemy within, such as the Pentagon, the State Department or the FBI, seemed more of a menace than the enemies without.

Secretary of Defence Robert Gates, a career CIA officer, had the experience, wisdom and knowledge to realise the horrendous complexities of the task of a DNI and sensibly refused the poisoned chalice. An effective DNI, an intelligence Tsar, would have to impose their will and leadership on this vast circus, taming egos, encouraging collegiate spirit and initiative, breaking down barriers between agencies and discouraging bureaucracy. The requirement was clear, but the problems were daunting. In February 2007 when McConnell accepted the job, he did so reluctantly, from a sense of duty. His dedication to duty was admirable: but the job is, in my view, impossible. Even in a police state where world and domestic opinion is of little significance and the dictator and their henchmen are above the law, the life of an intelligence supremo is not for the faint-hearted. Lavrenty Beria, chief of the NKVD, the Soviet intelligence agency, achieved some degree of coordination through terror, but in the process he became so hated and feared by his comrades in the Politburo that, as soon as Joseph Stalin, supremo of the Soviet Union, was dead they arranged for his arrest and execution.

No commercial organisations have ever had to manage, motivate and inspire such vast numbers scattered over so wide an area, though private military and security companies, some of which employ thousands of people, are likely to become increasingly involved in intelligence activities. Civilian government agencies may try to imitate the commercial world by attempting to measure performance by reference to targets, but such tools are difficult to apply in the intelligence world. It is bogus science to put numbers on intelligence results: the budgets are easily established, the results difficult to quantify. When it comes to cross border cooperation the image of the tower of Babel springs to mind; egos, national pride, competing agencies, many languages, differing cultures and religions can all play a role, some positive, some a hindrance.

The benefits of international cooperation in intelligence, such as the sharing of resources, are undoubtedly substantial, and continue to encourage cooperation. However, international liaison must be treated with care, and creates challenges of coordination. The two services involved represent two different nations and each may exploit liaison channels to make points in their national interest. A particular danger arises when a liaison service receives aid from a 'big brother' service. The recipient of aid will be tempted to exaggerate threats in order to loosen big brother's purse strings.

The Iraqi WMD case provided a good example of the difficulty faced by the US, in this instance of validating the product of a liaison source. In 1998 the German foreign intelligence service (the BND) had recruited an Iraqi chemical engineer who had wandered in to a refugee camp. The agent, codename CURVEBALL, provided material on the subject of chemical warfare, and on the Iraqi regime's chemical warfare capabilities. The BND shared the material with US intelligence, but would not allow US officers to meet the source. The material was detailed, and CIA analysts found it scientifically and technically sound. In October 2002, by which time CURVEBALL's material had assumed considerable importance, a CIA officer was despatched to press the BND for access to the source. The BND refused and went on to say it was suspected that he may have had a breakdown and even that he was perhaps fabricating intelligence. CURVEBALL himself has since publicly admitted that nearly everything he told the BND was false. The CURVEBALL example demonstrates that international coordination does not only involve the sharing of intelligence, but complex inter-agency relationships.

The British solution: The Joint Intelligence Committee

There were already coordination problems in Britain in the nineteenth century when communications started to move beyond the limits of horse or sailing ship, to steam and cable. The speed and variety of modern communications has changed the world. Good communication, however, does not guarantee interdepartmental collaboration. Nor does good communication solve the problem of winnowing out, recognising and highlighting nuggets of significant intelligence: it increases the problem by vastly increasing the amount of 'chaff' among which the gems are hidden. Despite these challenges, coordination is important and worthwhile. The members of the intelligence circus each have their strengths, and without pooling these the maximum benefit from this investment of resources cannot be gained. The British solution to coordination is the Joint Intelligence Committee, of which I was Secretary from 1968–72. The excellent first volume of its official history was published in 2014.[1]

The JIC's role embraces customer and assessor, and it is also the intelligence 'top table', looking across the board at intelligence issues, and advising government as appropriate. It has no department behind it, only a committee room in the Cabinet Office and a small supporting staff of seconded officers. As a customer it receives reports from all sources. It is the apex of the British assessment machinery, contributing to the final drafting process and approving, before circulation, the work of the assessments staff. As the intelligence top table it provides a unique forum for clearing ideas and avoiding friction between agencies. The JIC is a uniquely British institution, operating by consensus and guided by good sense and good manners. It is the envy of foreign counterparts who find that interdepartmental collaboration is not easy to achieve by command.

The JIC developed during the twentieth century, evolving from military origins to an all-purpose intelligence committee. Its members include the heads of the intelligence agencies, senior members of the armed services and senior policymakers from the Ministry of Defence, Foreign and Commonwealth Office, Cabinet Office, Home Office and Treasury. The Chairman has usually been a very senior individual holding a job in the Foreign Office, and the Deputy Chairman was, in my time, the Director-General of Defence Intelligence. All the JIC's members had full-time jobs outside the committee. The intelligence agencies did not take orders from the Committee or its Chairman.

The JIC was rarely in the limelight until the saga of the dossier on Iraq's alleged WMD (see Chapter Ten). Agencies have been faced with disgruntled officers blowing whistles; civil servants have taken a high moral position; Russian spies have been uncovered. All such titbits are meat and drink to the headline writers, but the doings of the interdepartmental committee are not. The British press had fare to offer that was far more interesting to most of its readers. The JIC's business was not about James Bond-like operations, but about assessments, most probably concerning some country of little interest to the public. If someone on the JIC staff seduced a secretary, or took a drink in the office during working hours, the press never knew.

The JIC's minutes had to be produced and circulated within twenty-four hours of each meeting, and so were written without consulting the members of the JIC. The Committee's product was notoriously dry. In the JIC Secretariat we prided ourselves on capturing the spirit of the debate and recording what the members had intended to say rather than what they had actually said. Personalities and verbatim quotes were anathema, and sensitive detail went into secret annexes. In the course of three-and-a-half years I only had two challenges to the minutes. The first was a light hearted tease by my Irish Deputy Chairman who said, 'those minutes of yours last week Brian, were not a record of the meeting that I attended.' The second challenge was serious; a member who had spoken long and learnedly at the previous meeting was not pleased to find that his masterpiece had been condensed to, '[i]n the course of the discussion the following point was made.' His protest was noted but the minutes were not changed.

A general criticism by outsiders was that our minutes were boring and our reports over fond of the 'on the one hand, but on the other' formula. But it was not the job of the assessment staff to make wild guesses or predictions. The JIC output was creditable in relation to the small staff involved, and remarkable considering the large staffs with which it was competing across the Atlantic.

The post of Intelligence Coordinator was created in 1968. Sir Dick White, the first Coordinator, whom I served for over three years as a staff officer, did not imagine that we were in command. I doubt if Sir Burke Trend, the Cabinet Secretary of the time, had any illusions about the reality either. I have known several of the British Intelligence Coordinators, and listened to Sir David Omand, former Security and Intelligence Coordinator (a post created in 2002), speak eloquently, and know that he has won golden opinions from his colleagues. I wonder, however, whether he found it much easier to coordinate independent agencies in the 2000s than we did in the 1970s.

The intelligence community that came closest to effective coordination may have been that which came to its full flowering under General Sir Gerald Templer during the Malayan Emergency of 1948–60 (see Chapter One). Templer had the temperament, the background, experience and staff, and he also had the authority, wearing the hats of High

Commissioner and Director of Operations, to impose his will on civilians and soldiers alike.

When Sir Maurice Oldfield became coordinator of security intelligence in Northern Ireland his first report conceded the unintended existence of two principal jobs: the first to oil the wheels of the intelligence machine; the second to blot up the blood spilt in the arguments between those participating in the intelligence effort. I had in fact, as Secretary of the JIC, tried to do the same thing in minor key. Like Oldfield later, I did my best to oil wheels. Although my Whitehall colleagues probably thought of me as an ex-colonial officer, specialising in Oriental affairs, my earlier experiences as a soldier stationed in Northern Ireland, and as a colleague of the government forces fighting the communists in Malaya, had equipped me with some knowledge of subjects relevant to 'the Troubles'. I clashed with Whitehall conventions when I introduced the Director of Special Branch, Royal Ulster Constabulary (RUC), to our Whitehall committee. My initiative, which seemed to have the merit of common-sense behind it, was not welcome. It was disappointing to meet the petty-mindedness of some Whitehall departments; but it was of course a similar attitude to the one which accompanied the recommendations by the JIC Far East that the Director of the Malayan Security Service should not be invited to join the Committee lest his views be too parochial. The Director of SB, RUC, was grudgingly allowed to attend. I hope that introducing him was at least useful in educating the Whitehall members, who knew little of Northern Ireland and had never been there.

I pointed out to my Whitehall colleagues that I had seen all this before in Malaya: the police were outnumbered and demoralised there. The situation in Northern Ireland was similar: we had abolished the RUC's auxiliary force (the B Specials) and were reducing the number of British troops. My colleagues were appalled and told me that I was a bad old colonialist. Alas I was right; when the lid came off the kettle there were not enough forces of law and order to put it back on again. I took no pleasure from the fact that I was right. It was a classic example of wishful thinking and complacency.

A problem facing any coordinator of intelligence is watertight compartments, which can too easily prevent an essential interchange of intelligence. In my JIC days I had been led to believe that the need to separate collection from intelligence requirements and analysis of intelligence was fully established. But the distinction was watered down in the pursuit of economy. The dossier on WMD in Iraq might have looked significantly different if this separation of functions had been properly monitored. A case officer without technical background will not be able to make an expert judgement on the plausibility of the reporting, and independent judgement must be brought to bear, to guard against agent handlers becoming overconfident about the reporting of their sources. The judgement must not be left to the case officer alone; there must be an independent arbiter.

Although the following sections of this chapter are separated into the categories of customers, and collectors, assessors and analysts, many of the points made in the latter are those that customers should also bear in mind.

The Customers

The ultimate customers and consumers of intelligence are the political masters who make policy decisions and their chief military advisers, and it is the function of intelligence to support these leaders. Leaders are seldom familiar with intelligence matters. President George Bush Snr was an exception: he had served as DCI for a short period. Consumers may have unrealistic expectations or underestimate intelligence. Kennedy lamented after the Bay of Pigs disaster that his experts had neither magic wand nor crystal ball. Tenet, DCI before 9/11, had been frustrated by the capacity of the US Government to ignore the urgency of the situation. Tenet said that 'the system was blinking red', but the politicians were not on high alert and nor did intelligence matters have top priority.

Failures of intelligence are often the fault not of the professional collectors and assessors, but of the customer who has chosen to ignore or reject inconvenient information. As the old saying goes, 'you can take a horse to the water but you cannot make it drink'. Sometimes they may decide that despite new inconvenient intelligence, an operation must be carried out as planned. A military case in point is the decision of the commanders in Operation Market Garden in 1944 to proceed with the airborne operation in the Netherlands despite the unwelcome last minute intelligence acquired by air photography about the arrival of a Panzer Division in the dropping zone. The airborne forces had been brought to an advanced state of readiness and delay was felt to be unacceptable.

The customers cannot be forced to give weight to inconvenient information. But there are none so deaf as those who choose not to hear. History has provided many examples of customers rejecting inconvenient intelligence. The job of the intelligence community is not finished until the customer has been persuaded to take notice.

Collectors and Assessors

The principal job of the collectors, in whatever agency they work, is to respond to the intelligence requirements of the policymakers. The collectors' performance is relatively easily judged; have they, or have they not, succeeded in obtaining the raw material needed to meet the intelligence requirements? Their performance should be judged against reasonable criteria: intelligence officers do not, as Helms said, possess divine wisdom, and there is no tool available to unlock all the secrets of the human mind. Moreover, since no agency has access to unlimited resources, it is impossible for them to monitor the globe at all times, though international intelligence liaison can help to some extent.

The assessors' function is to judge the reliability, accuracy and significance of the material provided to them by the collectors and analysts, and then to draft papers based on all sources for the customers. There is no doubt that the assessors' job comes with great responsibility. The assessors are generalists: they depend on specialists, including those in the defence intelligence community, for technical and scientific analysis. There was, it seemed to me during my years in the JIC, a tendency to keep science and technology out of the debate. I was not very popular with the traditionalists when I introduced specialists into our meetings. The recriminations after the Iraqi WMD affair suggest that we are still guilty of keeping the scientific analysts out of the debate.

Intelligence Requirements

If the intelligence community is to be the servant of the government it should concentrate on the targets and priorities set by the government, known in the Anglophone community as the 'requirements'. They must also, however, maintain a state of grace so they can respond to the unexpected. The list of requirements set out by the JIC, after consultation with all their customers, only reflected the past and the present; the items were broad brush and they certainly were not based on some fortune teller's globe. The vast majority of the requirements were obvious to any intelligent, experienced officer with expertise in the area to which he or she was being posted. This reduced the JIC list to little more than a checklist of immediate interests. Further, they were too extensive for a single agency to cover by themselves. They were an important but not exhaustive list of all the points upon which the customers at any particular moment in time might seek enlightenment from intelligence collection. So to treat the JIC requirements as though they were the only subjects to consider was to make a serious error. Intelligence officers were employed to do more than tick boxes: a good SIS officer in the field should use imagination and local knowledge to peer into the future and to pinpoint new requirements which had not yet been identified by Whitehall.

In the case of the Falklands War, the intelligence community was not formally tasked to focus on the intentions of Argentina's President Leopoldo Galtieri, and the British Ambassador and his Defence Attaché's warnings of the danger were waved airily aside by the apparatchiks in Whitehall. The magnificent victory over the Argentinian invaders distracted attention from the failure of all concerned to focus on the threat. The criticisms in the Falkland Islands Review, completed by the Franks Committee in 1983, were so gently worded that they were rapidly forgotten, even if they were understood. No-one had doubted that the Falklands were a problem, but no-one had a solution that would square the circle, meeting the demands of Argentinian *amour-propre*, while satisfying the democratic demands of a small sheep farming community thirty days sailing from their motherland. So the government did not seek reminders about the Falklands from intelligence channels.

The Afghan problem was of a different order of magnitude in terms of its impact on world affairs. Afghanistan has long been a cockpit and seldom been at peace. In the nineteenth and early twentieth centuries British India and Russia strove to extend their influence in Afghanistan. British India never achieved satisfactory, friendly relations with Afghanistan. The Russians too failed.

It certainly was a great mistake to remove Afghanistan entirely from the list of intelligence priorities the moment the Russians departed the country in 1989. The US Embassy and the CIA station there were closed. Afghanistan, in so far as it was studied at all, became the responsibility of CIA's Near Eastern Division, based at CIA Headquarters in Langley, Virginia. The Islamabad CIA station's directive contained no mention of Afghanistan, and the only active CIA work in that country was concerned with the hunt for Mir Aimal Kansi, the angry young man who had killed or wounded several CIA staff on the morning of 25 January 1993 as they were driving to work.

There is no way of proving that the situation would have been significantly better had the intelligence tap not been turned off as soon as the Russians withdrew. But surely the CIA might have been able to afford and support a mini station in Kabul? A tiny team to monitor, analyse and try to understand the post-Soviet developments. Over a decade later, the cost of such an intelligence operation looks negligible when compared with the cost in cash and lives of our attempts to help the Afghanis. The US had declared a victory and turned its attention elsewhere, and the consequences remain with us a generation later.

Getting requirements roughly right, in terms of current situations, is relatively easy. Ensuring that the requirements reflect future dangers is much less easy, and Afghanistan provides a painful example of the problems that can arise if the international players are over-addicted to short-termism. Intelligence collectors must not only look at the formal requirements, they should also look at matters which are not yet included in the formal list.

Training and Education

Human resources are key to intelligence organisations, but I defy anyone to be precise about what makes a good intelligence officer. I have known many admirable people in the profession, and they have come in all shapes and sizes and with differing characteristics. As a general proposition, I suggest that there are few jobs which are in greater need of people with drive, conscience, sense of national duty and initiative who are also quick learners, brave, responsible and able to work alone. Such qualities are desirable for intelligence officers, but most are also desirable in other careers.

Once good people are selected and recruited, it is of vital importance that they receive appropriate training and education. In the Cold War period the Soviets considered that spymasters required a long training that combined a broad education of a university style and specialist training. The journal compiled and smuggled out of the Soviet Union by Colonel Oleg Penkovsky, the GRU (Soviet military intelligence service) officer who spied for the West, is particularly informative on the matter of training. According to Penkovsky the GRU training organisations included a diplomatic academy, institutes for foreign languages, communications and intelligence, and schools for illegals (those who operate without official cover and without diplomatic immunity) and for diversion and sabotage.[2] The Soviet intelligence academies turned out many officers and I was told by an ex-KGB officer's wife that the Soviet services went in for matchmaking: wives were definitely part of the intelligence team.

The British services confine themselves to short, entry courses, where new recruits are taught the tricks of the trade before starting their apprenticeship in the field. In my time, training in the intelligence and security services was related to the methodology and techniques required to carry out the job. The courses did not range outside the nuts and bolts into the uses of intelligence and its value.

For those seeking confirmation that the cult of the amateur is not without merit, we can note with satisfaction the many British achievements in the intelligence and security fields during the Cold War. True, the Soviets had many successes, including deeply imbedded illegals, and ideologically and financially motivated sources. But the West had Oleg Gordievsky, the KGB officer spying for SIS and MI5, Penkovsky, and many others whose names are not publicly known.

Creating a British intelligence Staff College ought to be given serious consideration. Alternatively, intelligence high flyers who might be expected to reach senior ranks could be given a sabbatical year so they can read around the subject and engage in discussions with other members of the intelligence community. Such sabbaticals used to be given to diplomats in the Foreign and Commonwealth Office. This need not be expensive: universities already offer courses in intelligence studies, many of which are aimed at, and are taken up by, intelligence professionals.

University courses provide opportunities for serving or future intelligence officers to gain a formal, certified education in intelligence studies. Such courses draw students' attention to the value of intelligence and to the place of the intelligence officer's specific activities relative to wider intelligence practices. As argued elsewhere in the book, understanding the value and the context of intelligence is certainly a most desirable attribute for intelligence officers.

Without the opportunity to study the lessons of history in some depth, whether at university or in an intelligence Staff College, the intelligence officer cannot reasonably be expected to avoid errors already made by others. Since officers tend to be very busy on their day-to-day jobs, the likelihood is that they do not find time for research into the broader issues, so they learn by osmosis and personal reflection. Studying for an accredited degree provides the opportunity to engage directly with fellow students, many of whom will also be intelligence officers, and provides guidance on how to find one's way through the published literature on intelligence.

A handful of British universities already offer Masters degrees in intelligence studies.[3] Some of these are designed exclusively for the intelligence officer. These are studied remotely over the internet using online discussion boards accessible only to students and university staff. Increasing the links between the intelligence community and universities will help a greater proportion of intelligence officers become aware of this opportunity to learn about intelligence in the round and to learn the lessons of the past.

Conclusion

Intelligence requirements are a formal way in which the government tells the intelligence community what it needs. The US spent a great deal more time and effort than the UK did on trying to ensure that the list of requirements was complete. Yet this remains an unattainable goal: the world keeps changing. Requirements allow the government, who sit at the top of the intelligence chain, to feed their priorities back to the collectors, who are positioned at the bottom of this chain. Coordination is required in order to make the best possible use of the resources present at each stage of the chain. Formal coordination mechanisms such as the JIC, and the holders of posts such as the DNI and the UK's Intelligence and Security Coordinator, have numerous, difficult tasks. Coordination is important, but expectations must be realistic.

5

TYPES OF INTELLIGENCE COLLECTION METHODS

What follows does not aspire to be an exhaustive list of every method of intelligence collection or every ingredient in the assessment process. Nor do the types always fit neatly into tidy categories such as human intelligence (Humint) and technical intelligence (Techint). Signals intelligence (Sigint), for example, is collected by technical means but the material it collects requires human intervention to turn the raw product into useful intelligence. Yet it is convenient to have a short form name by which to refer to intelligence subjects. And it reminds us of the multiplicity of intelligence activities of varying degrees of importance, each of which has, on some occasion, made a significant contribution to the complex process of assembling the intelligence mosaic.

Language has changed in recent decades. What used to be known as overt intelligence is now often called open source intelligence (Osint). The classifications overt and covert are also open to debate. Some information, which is 'unclassified' in a democratic society and which the public may demand to see under Freedom of Information legislation, may well be treated as a state secret in an undemocratic state where officials and politicians can make their lives easier by minimising the flow of information to the general public. The intelligence community should always remember that overt information, much less glamorous than secret reports, has a vital part to play.

Not all the terms discussed in this chapter are universal currency. The transatlantic short forms like Trashint (trash intelligence), Rumint (rumour intelligence) and Hunchint (hunch intelligence) refer to sub-groups of collection methods that clearly do not compete with such categories as Sigint, Imint (imagery intelligence) and Audint (audio intelligence) in terms of the volume of intelligence they produce, but on occasion they have made seminal contributions. Even graffiti can be of interest. I once found myself in a Chinese urinal where extremely rude words had been painted on the walls calling into question Mao's parenthood and impugning his virility. Clearly there were still sparks of opposition to be found hidden under the drab clothes of the workers and peasants. In short, all sources may have some relevance and top secret code word material is not the only source of value.

Humint and Techint are not, of course, mutually exclusive; Techint, for example, requires vast human resources and may assist Humint. Both forms of intelligence are required. They are complementary, neither is necessarily better than the other, and the past enthusiasm of customers for Techint on the grounds that it was less likely to cause embarrassment than Humint was ill-founded. This has been demonstrated all too well by the embarrassment of western governments caused by whistleblower Edward Snowden's disclosures about their secret Techint collection activities. Embarrassment can also be caused when friends are found to be spying on friends, regardless of the methods used to do so. Every nation which has the ability almost certainly attempts to spy on its friends in order to have a better understanding of their true intentions.

Those who believed that Techint was less potentially embarrassing than Humint might also have remembered the case of Gary Powers and his U-2 photo reconnaissance aircraft, which was shot down by the Soviet Union in 1960, giving them a chance to put the pilot on trial and to rage against the US's spying activities. Additionally, the comforting idea that Techint is less likely than Humint to include an element of fabrication and deception may be true, but Techint can also mislead.

Admiral Stansfield Turner, who took over from Bush Snr as the Director of the CIA in the mid-1970s, was a Techint aficionado. He had been head of the NSA, the US Sigint agency, and knew the value of Sigint. Yet he clearly had not read much intelligence history or he would have known that communications are often used for deception purposes, or that, although the camera does not lie, the objects it photographs may be fabrications. And as to the reliability of intercepted documents, there are many cases where skilfully created documents have fooled leading experts. Britain had major successes in this field in both World Wars.

The attack on Pearl Harbor provided some excellent lessons on the limits of Techint, which Turner does not seem to have learnt. The long radio silence of the Japanese Navy resulted in there being no clue as to the Japanese positioning in the days before its attack on Pearl Harbor in December 1941. The Japanese were also extremely lucky to have heavy cloud cover to conceal their vast armada. In this case there was no Humint to help since the Japanese had prevented foreign attachés from visiting the areas where the fleet was perfecting its bombing techniques and assembling. There was a third Techint problem in the last hour before the attack. When the young radar operator at Pearl Harbor found his radar screen filled with images of a swarm of aircraft and reported the fact to his superior, he was told not to worry as they must be US planes. Turner and his fellow technical enthusiasts might have pondered the fact that in this case Sigint was deaf, cameras blind, and radar signals were misread.

So both categories of intelligence collection methods are essential and complementary, neither is necessarily available when required, and both can cause embarrassment. In any case, however many brilliant new technical methods are developed, good human agents will still be necessary, if only to interpret information about the minds of the enemy leadership and the state of morale, training, and so on. Satellite photography can produce results that no human agent could, but the human agent can produce the background knowledge to enable the analysts to perform effectively when assessing images taken by satellite. Agents' background knowledge can help analysts to address questions of quality, training and experience, and to predict intention. Techint may tell us what the enemy is saying and doing; it cannot tell us their intentions.

Human Intelligence (Humint)

Q 'I am always preceded by a hundred spies.'

Frederick the Great of Prussia, c.1757

'One spy in the right place is worth 20,000 men in the field.'

Attributed to Napoleon Bonaparte

'[t]he laws of the universe can be verified by mathematical calculation: but the dispositions of an enemy are ascertainable through spies and spies alone.'

Mei Yao-chen commenting on Sun Tzu's 'The Art of War', eleventh century[1]

'I will never again command an army in America if we must carry along paid spies.'

General William T. Sherman, US Army, 1863

'You can send your "source" from the German air force to his whore of a mother! This is not a "source" but a disinformer.'

Joseph Stalin, 1941

There have been attempts to compare the value of human intelligence with technical intelligence. There is no point in such an exercise as both are essential elements in intelligence work. For example, aerial photography can cover vast areas of ground in seconds, which a human agent could not cover in a lifetime. However, human agents are required to steal the plans and interpret intentions. In this section the prominent types of Humint sources are discussed, namely the use of agents, walk-ins and defectors, as well as less discussed types including exile intelligence and rumour intelligence.

Agents

'One who does not employ local guides will not secure advantages of terrain.'

Sun Tzu, 'The Art of War', fifth century BC

'People suitable as special agents … are 20 to 45 years old. Persons from aristocratic and bourgeois-conservative circles are of no interest. … People who adhere strictly to church dogma and rules are not suitable, nor are people with a tendency toward alcoholism, drug addiction, and or sexual deviations.'

KGB Handbook on recruitment of agents

'Your … spy must be a man of keen intellect, though in outward appearance a fool; of shabby exterior, but with a will of iron. He must be active, robust, endowed with physical strength and courage: thoroughly accustomed to all sorts of dirty work, able to endure hunger and cold, and to put up with shame and ignominy.'

Tu Mu, a commentator on Sun Tzu, eighth or ninth century

'He who lacks wisdom cannot use agents; he who is not humane and generous cannot direct agents; he who is not sensitive and alert cannot get the truth out of them.'

Sun Tzu, 'The Art of War', fifth century BC

What sorts of people make good spies? Although most of the best-known spies have been men, there have also been highly successful women (the unfortunate Mata Hari was not among them). Probably the only characteristic shared by all successful spies is their ability to dissemble and deceive. Their motives are varied and include greed, disappointment, bruised egos, failure in the promotion stakes, talents that went unrecognised, disillusionment and a desire for revenge. In some cases they may respond to a case officer's flattery and sympathy. They may be ripe for development by a case officer who appears to recognise their virtues. Some may simply be grateful to find a friend. Others may be seriously disenchanted with the system in their country and anxious to promote change.

Even from a well-motivated agent with excellent access, we must not expect miracles. Although Rumsfeld's phrase 'unknown unknowns', which refers to things 'we don't know we don't know', has been mocked, he made an important point. It is impossible to direct an agent on to targets you do not know exist. Here we are in the business of logical fallacies and philosophical quandaries. That you have failed to find something does not prove that the object you are looking for does not exist.

There is another basic problem: even if your agent obtains the minutes of the latest Cabinet meeting, the decisions recorded can be changed at any moment. If there had been an Abwehr (German military intelligence) agent at General Eisenhower's meetings in early June 1944, the agent would only have been able to report that the invasion of Normandy might have to be postponed because of bad weather. Eisenhower decided to go ahead at the last minute, deeply worried. He might as easily have decided to postpone. So we are brought back to the ineluctable truth: that no-one can foretell the future with absolute certainty.

Clearly a reliable spy with good access is a pearl beyond price and the best are likely to be motivated by something more noble than greed. Penkovsky and Gordievsky did not work for the West for money, but because they had become disillusioned with Communism. Even reliable agents may forget, mishear, misjudge or misinterpret, or be over-eager to please. These are weaknesses to which a technical device is not prone.

Moreover, even if the original motivation of the recruit was shared values, ideology, and friendship, the agent may have second thoughts about betraying the motherland, or be turned, by blackmail for example, into a double agent.

Close friendly relationships with agents have special problems. Handovers are not supposed to be dependent on personal chemistry. This ideal tidy view of agent handling does not, unfortunately, fit reality; an agent working for money alone may have little interest in the personality of their new case officer, but others may not wish to be reminded that he or she is technically a spy to be handed on to a new case officer. The topics that follow remind us that there is nothing simple about the intelligence business.

Walk-ins and defectors

Defectors are of many different sorts. They may be agents who have lost their access or be in danger, or people who have never before been in contact with a foreign intelligence service and decide to 'walk in' to offer their services. But 'walk-ins' may be the agents of the local security service. Is it a trap? Is it a provocation intended to stir up diplomatic trouble? And is it sufficiently promising to justify the expenditure of huge resources and risk a diplomatic protest? While the potential host government is mulling over the case, the clock is ticking, the enemy may have rumbled the volunteer and already put them under full surveillance.

Gordievsky's case was a resounding success for him and for British intelligence who helped him to escape the net. After beginning work for SIS in 1974, the KGB only began to suspect him in 1985. SIS helped Gordievsky escape the Soviet Union and defect to Britain. Sadly, in the Penkovsky case, the Soviets arrested him and wreaked a bloody revenge.

Twice during my time in Beijing I was summoned in the middle of the night by the Head of Mission to deal with Chinese citizens who had climbed over the compound wall and presented themselves to the startled British security guard. Each time I concluded that they had nothing to offer that was likely to persuade the British Government that they were worth the untold problems which would have arisen had we allowed them to stay on British soil. So, wishing them luck, they were hoisted back across the compound wall. The Chinese authorities never mentioned either of the incidents so we had no idea whether these were genuine would-be escapees with excellent night movement skills or failed agents provocateurs.

Exile intelligence (Exint)

Exiles are tricky. They may be more vulnerable to the blackmail of their mother country's secret services than to the blandishments of Western intelligence services. One of the most successful operations mounted by any secret service in the twentieth century was the brilliant infiltration of the Russian émigré clubs by the Russian revolutionary secret service, the Cheka, in an operation in the 1920s named Trest. An analogous situation arose when the KMT evacuated China in 1948 and moved to Taiwan. The KMT's intelligence service and nationalist exiles were an attractive target for the West, but they were frequently under the control of the Communist security apparatus.

The temptation to liaise with the KMT was strong but many intelligence officers were badly misled by their KMT contacts about the state of affairs in China. The KMT took with it to Taiwan a vast apparatus of intelligence security officers and on the face of it they were much better placed than Western agencies to collect intelligence about mainland China. The problem of sifting the true from the false was formidable, since Western intelligence officers could not operate in the People's Republic.

This China case illustrates another danger. The foreigners gratefully receiving the confidences of exiles seldom pause to wonder whether their opinions might be suspect since the exile had not been in their native country for decades and, perhaps, had seldom, if ever, ventured far from the capital cities. Nor were their foreign contacts inclined to question whether a good knowledge of English guaranteed reliable views. If the subject under discussion was plans for regime change, the agent might find it all too easy to agree rather than to point out difficulties. At the centre of the Exint problem is the fact that an exile has little or nothing to lose if an invasion fails, and much to gain if the attack succeeds.

Heavy reliance on Exint arises when a target country has become a closed police state, making it difficult for people to travel freely across its borders. In a police state with strict border controls it is difficult, if not impossible, for intelligence officers to visit the country to talent spot, recruit and run agents or to verify agent reporting through personal observation on the ground. At a time when the country concerned may have become a top priority intelligence target and more sources are required, the intelligence officer's opportunity to check on the bona fides of potential sources will have become severely limited. The exile community may look attractive but their reliability is difficult to judge.

The failed invasion of Cuba at the Bay of Pigs provides a seminal example of the problem of discovering the truth about the strength of opposition to a dictatorship when the agent base consists almost entirely of exiles. Cubans exiled in Florida offered a convenient quarry for the CIA's agent recruitment efforts, but even if they had genuine sub-sources in Cuba there was a problem of bias. The Cuban sources were anti-Castro and had a vested interest in encouraging the US to support a regime change. It is surprising that given its importance, intelligence from exiles is rarely discussed in the literature. It is a source that should be treated with great care.

Hunch intelligence (Hunchint)

Hunchint challenges accepted views. It should not be dismissed out of hand when it is produced by experienced professionals. In these cases the analysts and assessors should look at the evidence afresh. Such interpretations of the evidence are not always recognised as the potentially significant warnings that they may be. Perhaps the best-known case of Hunchint is DCI John A. McCone's hunch about the Soviets' weapons deployments in Cuba in 1962. There was no hard intelligence, secret or otherwise to support his hunch that the Soviets would exploit their relationship with the Cubans to the full and deploy Medium-Range Ballistic Missiles (MRBMs). But the photographs taken by a U-2 plane proved that he was right. Clearly assessments cannot be changed on the basis of hunches, but when the people who question the conclusion on the basis of their 'gut feelings' have a long, distinguished and relevant career behind them, their hunches should not be ignored.

Trash intelligence (Trashint)

The late Sir Reginald Hibbert, a diplomat whom I had known since my Oxford days, used to complain to me that the restrictions on taking intelligence material home after work made it difficult to give that material as much attention as it deserved. Not all officials obeyed those tedious rules. The intelligence gained from rubbish bins, wastepaper baskets and other forms of detritus would be a very minor part of collecting intelligence if everyone were fully security conscious. Fortunately for intelligence collectors, people are careless. The trash of offices and residences have always provided rich pickings and in the twenty-first century people who may remember to deal securely with paper may easily forget the vulnerability of their personal computer.

A well-documented case demonstrating the value of Trashint is that of Aldrich Ames, the CIA officer who spied for the KGB from the mid-1980s to the 1990s. It was Trashint which first confirmed that he was a spy. A fifty-strong FBI team had failed to find hard evidence. Two tiny pieces of crumpled paper and the records in his computer provided conclusive evidence of his treachery. Although Ames was a CIA officer trained in the arts of intelligence and security, he failed dismally to perform according to the CIA's elementary security rules.

Cab intelligence (Cabint)

The use of taxi drivers as a source is a standing joke among intelligence professionals and journalists, but there is something serious to be said about it. The taxi driver plying their trade in a war zone has considerable opportunity to observe the local scene, and, since his life depends upon avoiding trouble, a strong motive for making an accurate assessment of the situation. Unlike most embassy staff the taxi driver speaks the local language and is unhampered by the sort of strict security arrangements imposed by governments on their employees. They have the motivation to gather intelligence, and access denied to most foreign observers trapped within security compounds. Conversing with taxi drivers is therefore one way to collect intelligence that can help improve understanding of the mood and general attitude within a country, region or city.

Rumour intelligence (Rumint)

'Rumint' describes anything being discussed by the general public. It should not be totally ignored. Although, like Hunchint, it is no substitute for properly sourced intelligence, the average person in the street or in the bazaar has a good motive for thinking about the local political and economic situation, and has their ear closer to the ground than any foreigner. Rumint may be a pointer to future events and a useful trigger for investigation.

Neither the Indian Mutiny in the nineteenth century nor the Burmese Army's coup d'état in the twentieth, were foreseen. But Rumint gave some lead-time. In the Indian case rumours in the bazaar of impending mutiny were well founded. Unfortunately many officers with long service in India had blind faith in the loyalty of their courageous troops, so the Rumint was often ignored and British officers paid the penalty. In Burma, now known as Myanmar, in 1958 we had an analogous, but from the British perspective a less significant situation, when the bazaar was flooded with rumours of an Army coup d'état. We had no hard evidence to support the rumours but at least we listened and had time to prepare for trouble.

I was not in Beijing in 1966 when the Red Guards attacked the embassy and the consulate general in Shanghai but I assume that in both cases the Red Guards got out of hand, so there was no scope for pre-warning. In any case, Rumint was hard to come by in the China of those days. Coffee shopping with locals was not an option and local staff did not swap gossip with us.

The purist may reject out of hand the idea that such grey areas should be seriously considered. To them I would suggest that intelligence assessments must include contemplation of all possibilities. Conclusions should obviously be based on hard fact if possible, but 'all sources' should include rumours carefully qualified. A rumour may turn out to be correct, while a report from an agent's sub source may turn out to be a deception, an embroidery, a gullible mistake, caused perhaps by a desire to please the case officer. As with interrogation, and whether information extracted by what can be called torture can be trusted, so with Rumint. The answer is 'of course not'; it must be set against the whole picture.

Technical Intelligence (Techint)

'I believe the country needs this information, and I'm going to approve it [the U-2 programme]. But I'll tell you one thing. Some day one of these machines is going to be caught, and then we'll have a storm.'

President Eisenhower, 1954

'Intercepted communications could be a more promising source of intelligence if it weren't for our national tendency to logorrhea about the subject.'

R. James Woolsey, former DCI, 2002

This section of the chapter would be long indeed if it attempted even the most summary description of the technical developments of the last century. Scientific and technical aids to intelligence gathering have exploded in the developed world, including the huge efforts put into Research and Development in two world wars, during the Cold War, and since. The slow, wood and cloth built biplanes and triplanes, dropping bombs by hand, soon evolved into the Spitfire and long-range bombers of the Second World War, and thence to supersonic planes and to aerial platforms for electronic warfare systems, and more recently to the Predator, an unmanned aerial vehicle (UAV) or 'drone' carrying weapons and cameras, while satellites float in space. The mobile phone has replaced the clumsy Bakelite telephone, tethered to its copper wire. The heavy wooden camera and its plates moved rapidly on to miniature spy cameras and digital cameras. The Bletchley Park computer of the Second World War has morphed into a household gadget that packs more punch than the Bletchley model; tablets are multi-functional and easily transported, and huge amounts of data can be stored cheaply. The radio has advanced from whiskers and crystals, through valves, and solid state to digital, and the first clumsy wire recorders have become tiny pocket tape recorders.

Until the industrial revolution little changed in the intelligence world. The spy and his messages could travel faster on a train than on a horse, and more reliably on a steam driven boat than a sailing ship, but there was no change in basic methodology. The scientific and technical revolution of the twentieth century on the other hand, has opened up entirely new areas. The explosion of new technologies has been as far reaching in its effect on intelligence as it has been in the wider military and civilian world.

Every technical advance that is likely to benefit a collector of intelligence will provide security officers, tasked with preventing information from reaching enemy hands, with a new headache. For example, the dry, portable, efficient copying machines which in the 1980s superseded a generation of slow and messy copiers were a godsend not only to office staff but also to spies and so a nightmare for security officers. Or take the case of image intensifiers and infrared devices; a godsend certainly to poachers and to spies, able to capture images, which bad weather, the darkness, or good camouflage nets would have previously denied to them. Removing the cloak of darkness cuts both ways. The night is no longer a cloak for clandestine activity of any sort, and often security has been slow to recognise the full horror of the situation created by new gadgetry. It is highly convenient to be able to stick a beacon device onto a target's vehicle thus making it easy to follow the target wherever he moves; but the enemy too can acquire such gadgets and use them to monitor their opponents.

Technical intelligence, like human intelligence, has limitations and weaknesses. When the signals are not there to collect, Sigint has little to offer. Whatever advances are made in interception and cipher breaking, Siginters need some cooperation from their targets. Analogous limitations apply when collecting audio intelligence. However excellent the audio quality of the telephone tap or the microphone, it will avail the intelligence officer nothing if the targets follow the oppressive disciplines of good audio security: no 'shop' talk in hotel bedrooms or in offices unless they are specially constructed secure rooms; no 'shop' talk in restaurants or other public places which may have been fitted out with audio gadgetry; and no casual assumption that it is safe to talk in the garden where directional microphones, or even lip reading, may pose a danger. Well disciplined targets can frustrate the best technology. Not every ambassador is so careless as to speak on insecure phone lines in an insecure room; not every military commander so careless as to use insecure communications. At the moment when secret intelligence is most desirable, the sources may become silent.

The Complementary Nature of Techint and Humint

Until the development of electricity, there was no prospect of avoiding the messy uncertainties of Humint by using technology. Before then, the nearest we had got to Techint matters was the world of the 'black chambers' of the Western powers, where cryptography and secret writing were studied. Rulers had learnt to protect themselves from snoopers and eavesdroppers by such devices as creaking floorboards; the Chinese had developed a system for giving advance warning of enemy movement, by burying skin-covered drums in the ground which would respond to the sound of marching men before the sounds were audible to the sentries. But while the weapons of war and transport systems had made formidable advances, the weapons of intelligence were much the same as they always had been. Eyes, ears and brains were the weapons. The advent of electronics and the development of the optical sciences changed the scene dramatically; and now there are Techint weapons of enormous power.

It is understandable that governments might hope that a new technical dawn was breaking in the intelligence field. The magic which had been wrought by the Siginters in the Second World War, and the ability of an overhead camera to capture the image of a golf ball from 30,000 feet, soon led to unrealistic hopes that Techint could replace the use of agents and eliminate the potential for embarrassment which they represented. In military matters politicians would like to replace boots on the ground by technical devices, using military aircraft and naval vessels to deliver weapons from afar. So the idea of Predator-type aircraft to collect intelligence is attractive. But just as it has been found impossible in the military world to dispense with troops, so in the intelligence world it has been found that however wondrous science and technology, there is still a need for humans on the ground.

Even James R. Schlesinger, Helms' successor as DCI, who had no love for the CIA and its agents, understood that technology could not alone provide all the answers. His comment, '[y]ou cannot photograph an intention', encapsulates the ineluctable truth that, although it is indeed useful to have a full picture of the size and composition of a dictator's armed forces, it is also important to know what the dictator intends to do. And there are other reasons why the camera has limitations. In the case of aerial photography although the camera does not lie, the subjects it is photographing may have been created as part of a deception plan. In the case of ground photography it is not unknown for agents to fabricate; a combination of skilled photographer and expert model maker can produce extremely realistic images.

There is no guarantee that pouring money into the recruitment of spy masters and spies will solve all intelligence problems; but nor is there any guarantee that ever increasing expenditure on expensive technology will solve all the problems either. The appointment of Turner, formerly Director of NSA, to direct the CIA, was a reflection of Presidential frustrations with the uncertainties and potential embarrassments of traditional operations using agents. Turner naturally resented the criticism that he harmed the Agency by overemphasising technical means, and damaged morale among Humint officers, but the criticism has not been stilled.

Signals intelligence (Sigint)

Sigint is the descendant of the black chambers of Cardinal Richelieu of France and the Russian and British spymasters of the past who pored over intercepted messages. The explosion of communications based on the invention of electricity and then of computers and mobile phones has given Siginters more targets and more problems as the volume of messages grows ever larger. British mobile phone users, for example, send billions of text messages each year. The attack and the defence alike rely on ever more sophisticated computers; communicators seek an unbreakable system, and the Siginters strive to prove that the phrase 'unbreakable cipher' is an oxymoron. The battle between Siginters and communicators will continue. There will probably never be a totally secure system, but as the cost and delays involved in unbuttoning the latest systems escalate, a Sigint success may often be too late to affect the tactical situation.

Each type of intelligence collection method, from time to time, produces a gem, both all are susceptible to deception, and each has advantages and disadvantages. However, if one were to attempt to rank methods according to the impact their intelligence has had on world events, Sigint would come high on the list of technical means. Higher perhaps than satellite and aerial photography, which cannot tell us the reason for deployment. Sigint is a golden goose which can at times produce real time coverage of the very highest levels of communications.

Sigint's virtues are accompanied by a singular weakness. The immediacy and accuracy of an intelligence report based on Sigint make it relatively easy for security agencies to decide that a leak has emanated not from Humint, but from Sigint, and the immediate consequence is likely to be a change in the communications system, thus plugging the leak. By contrast, there may be hundreds of human suspects who might have had access to the information passed to the enemy, and there is unlikely to be a quick identification of the culprit however urgent and efficient the mole hunts. If an agent is blown, or a microphone found, there may be embarrassment, as well as a loss of intelligence; but in the case of Sigint if a country discovers that its supposedly unbreakable cipher has been mastered by its opponents, it can arrange to change the system worldwide, and thus suddenly deny the enemy, possibly at a crucial moment, all access to top level communications.

A similar situation arose in the interwar period when the British Government's fears of the subversive activities of the Soviet communist agitators led Stanley Baldwin's Government to reveal to the Soviets that they were reading their cables and knew all about their nefarious activities, fomenting and funding unrest. The result, inevitably, was that the Soviets ceased providing the British code breakers with material, and turned to written communication by diplomatic bag.

British successes in attacking German communications during the Second World War are now well known. But it is less well known that there were many successes against other adversaries, including the Japanese, which presented special difficulties because of its three scripts: Romaji (romanised; used for their telegrams); Kanji (Chinese characters); and Kana (seventy phonetic symbols). Further, a Japanese dictionary might present more than thirty different choices under one Romaji entry. The Siginters did well.

There is another side to this discussion of the value of developing, maintaining and using a Sigint capability. An intelligence report based on Sigint is likely to be given exceptional credence and importance. There is no doubt that Sigint carries both the reputation of reliability, as well as the highest vulnerability. Although the customers are usually sensitive to such security matters, it is all too easy for them to forget the sources of their knowledge and thereby inadvertently betray them by giving hints to the opposition. Conversely, if the real provenance of a Sigint based report is concealed, it may lose its impact on the consumers of intelligence.

Imagery intelligence (Imint)

The technology of Imint has advanced by leaps and bounds over the last century, and the process has accelerated with the development of overhead photography from highflying aircraft and satellites. In the 1960s the U-2 and SR-71 programme developed reconnaissance aeroplanes that could fly sufficiently high that they were, it was hoped, beyond the range of the Soviet missiles of the time. Although U-2s were shot down over the Soviet Union, China and Cuba, the programme was hugely successful. This is best demonstrated by the pivotal role of the U-2 in dispelling the 'bomber gap' myth in 1956, reassuring the US that until then they had overestimated the capability of the Soviet air force. The successor programmes used satellites and were also successful. A CIA analyst calculated that the Corona satellite programme could provide more coverage in one capsule of exposed film returned to Earth than the U-2 programme could have provided in four years.

Meanwhile, photographic techniques have been developed that can overcome fog, cloud, darkness and smoke, and even, with heat sensors, defeat overhead covers and camouflage nets. Electronics enable cameras to take pictures around corners. However, there are limits to the capability of the camera. It cannot look into a cave or a subterranean shelter and the objects that it photographs may be deliberate deceptions. In addition, Imint does not speak for itself. It has to be interpreted and this introduces the possibility of human error. Nonetheless, images have provided valuable intelligence and will continue to do so.

Audio intelligence (Audint)

'Electronic intercepts are great, but you don't know if you've got two idiots on the phone.'

Martin Peterson, senior CIA analyst, 2000

'It's nothing but an eight-storey microphone plugged into the Politburo.'

Richard Amery, US Representative, describing the new
US Embassy building in Moscow

Audint can be extremely useful, producing instant intelligence that reflects the current thinking and views of the target. But it is difficult to get a microphone into the right place, especially as the danger of eavesdropping becomes ever more well known. Audint's potential is much greater than it should be because people tend to forget warnings only to use safe rooms when speaking, to turn on water taps, and so on to thwart the eavesdropper. Eavesdropping can be by a microphone in a wall or everyday object, or by a directional microphone which can enable an eavesdropper to hear a conversation at a considerable distance in the open air. Boring holes in walls and listening from next door is as old as history.

The reports of foreign visitors—business people and diplomats—saying that they know that they were 'bugged' have to be taken with a pinch of salt. Even a country with a population as large as China would be hard-pressed to cover every foreign visitor's hotel bedroom or conference room, record conversations, translate, process and promptly deliver a report. The use of Audint in court is quite a separate issue. The intelligence community, unlike the police, collects intelligence in order to find out the truth, not in order to produce evidence acceptable in court.

The new US Embassy in Moscow, for which building work began in 1979, was generously wired for sound by the KGB during the course of construction, and it was said that the walls were as full of holes as a Gorgonzola cheese. The US was, however, well used to the KGB's habits having long before discovered a microphone neatly concealed in the coat of arms fixed on the wall behind the Ambassador's desk. Nonetheless the skills of the audio specialist can be nullified if the targets are security conscious, stay away from places which may have been bugged, and conduct their conversations in open spaces beyond the range of directional microphones and lip readers.

Documentary intelligence (Docint)

'Reading a man's correspondence is not the same thing as reading his mind.'

Peter Calvocoressi, historian, 1979, cited in Philip Knightley, 'The Second Oldest Profession: The Spy as Bureaucrat, Patriot, Fantasist and Whore', 1986

For obvious reasons documents are highly valued sources of intelligence. But, as already remarked, there are such things as forgeries and some of these have fooled eminent historians. Once, when staying in a room in a South East Asian country normally occupied by an enemy officer, I found the draft treaty of a singularly unhelpful secret agreement between the government of the hosts and the enemy in a dressing table drawer. The draft was written in a language I could read quite readily. It has never become clear whether this was an accident or a deliberate gift from the local hosts whose sympathies lay with Britain. Either way it is an unusual and interesting example of luck. One potential problem with documents, however, is that they are the most obvious way of attempting to deceive the enemy. Examples where forged documents were used by the British with great success are described in the chapter on Deception Operations.

Open Source Intelligence

Osint does not fit neatly into either Humint or Techint. It could be electronic, it could be a printed page, it could be a radio broadcast. It is clearly not true that all the information required to make a good intelligence assessment is to be found in open source material. However, an energetic trawl of newspapers, radio and TV material can produce very useful background to a case or issue. For example, in the run up to the Argentine invasion of the Falklands, it would not have been difficult, by scrutinising the local press, to gauge the attitude and dangerous paranoia of Argentinian dictator President Galtieri. Not every nation publicises its intentions in so convenient a fashion, but in any society, even the most strictly censored police state, a great deal can be learnt from studying the media, by noting who is in and who is out in the leadership, by studying the changes in propaganda themes, and by reading between the lines, working out what has been left out and why. Tribute should be paid to the brilliant work done by the BBC Monitoring Service recording foreign broadcasts.

The intelligence services share with diplomats, journalists and academics the duty to seek the truth. All need to be constantly aware of the need to consult open official and unofficial material. The arrival of the great *Times* correspondent in the Crimean War prompted the Tsar of Russia to remark that, '[w]e have no need of spies. We have the *Times*.' In November 1941 *The Daily Telegraph* warned its readers of the likelihood of Japanese military retaliation against Western restrictions. The *Telegraph* reporting was closer to the mark than the official reports which allowed the US and Western governments to bury their heads in the sand before the Japanese attack on Pearl Harbor. Once when attending a lunch hosted by DCI Helms and emboldened, no doubt, by the stiff dry Martini which had preceded our teetotal meal, I asked our host which newspaper he recommended for a general conspectus of foreign affairs. He gave me his recommendation, adding that he always read that before looking at official papers. I would have liked to pursue the topic further but looking round the table I realised that this topic was not popular with officers who struggled daily to ensure that the DCI received the CIA's view of the world before breakfast.

There is no simple answer to the question of how to ensure that open sources are given their proper weight in the assessment process. In twenty-five years working without the luxury of secret sources, I and many of my ex-colleagues found that open sources, coupled with experience could often produce useful assessments. The most remarkable of the open bulletins available on China after I was no longer privy to classified intelligence was a regular publication by the Jesuit Father Laszlo LaDany. He led a tiny posse of Chinese linguists who covered the provincial Chinese broadcasting scene and reported usefully on internal affairs in that vast country at a time when no foreigner could roam around observing the scene. His product was extraordinary.

When working in the Cabinet Office, I always started the morning by skimming the Dublin and Belfast newspapers and the New China News Agency (NCNA) bulletin; everyone else seemed to be waiting for the input from embassies or British official sources. Putting aside the time delay involved in waiting for the official verdict from our various government contacts, there was also the problem that our Whitehall machine was looking at the situation indirectly through the prism of other official agencies who might, or might not, have considered 'all sources' when making their reports.

On the morning that the Chinese and the Soviets started a battle over the demarcation of the Sino-Soviet boundary at the Ussuri River, I received a copy of the New China News Agency (NCNA) daily bulletin, which obligingly included photographs of the two armies in action, tanks and guns firing, and a thirty page analysis of the battle as the Chinese wanted the world to see it. My contribution to the meeting was not entirely appreciated as it somewhat contradicted the impression given by our embassies. Later I found that having the NCNA delivered to my house had caused a flutter in security circles when they noted that a member of the Cabinet Office staff was the regular recipient of a Communist Chinese news bulletin.

No-one challenges the statement that intelligence assessments should be based on all sources, but inevitably a newspaper report is less glamorous than a top secret report. When I served in embassies it was accepted that every morning the Ambassador should preside over a meeting of Chancery and other relevant officers where the questions of the day would be discussed. Media reporting would be included in the discussion. In some countries there was little or no secret intelligence and media sources were uniquely important. Although in overseas posts the importance of open sources was likely to be well recognised, there seemed to be no machinery in Whitehall to ensure that the intelligence community was making full use of open as well as restricted material.

It is important to pay more than lip service to the concept of all source reporting. At the very least Osint may give warning of a crisis before official channels have woken up; they can be important, giving advance warning of something which has yet to be reported on official channels, and give colour to official reporting. Despite the value of open sources, human nature may well ensure that overt intelligence seldom gets its due: secrets are more interesting.

Conclusion

This chapter has outlined the commonly-discussed methods of collecting intelligence, as well as some that receive much less attention in the intelligence world and in books about intelligence. All means of collecting intelligence are important: human and technical, secret and open. Human and technical sources complement each other, as do secret and open sources. While it is tempting to overlook the importance of open source material, intelligence professionals may continue to be inclined to do just this. Preconceptions of Humint as less reliable than intelligence collected through technical means, and of Techint as less likely to cause embarrassment should their activities be exposed, are also flawed and difficult to eradicate.

Perhaps the most important point to be made about this chain of intelligence which leads from collection to customer is that like every chain its strength is determined by the strength of the weakest link. The recruitment of an ace spy, the development of a new technology, and the decryption of an interesting complex code are admirable achievements. However, unless the end product can be presented in timely and persuasive fashion so that the customer not only reads the report but acts upon it, the intelligence effort has been a waste of time and money. The glamour goes to the producers, but the final impact on the policymakers will be achieved, in the British case, by the JIC. The JIC's prose may be grey, but its judgements are the best available and are likely to have the most influence on policymakers.

6

ASSESSMENT

PROBLEMS AND COMMON FALLACIES

'Know your enemy and know yourself and in a hundred battles you will not be in peril.'

Sun Tzu, 'The Art of War', fifth century BC

'[W]e must develop a far deeper knowledge of other people's culture, religion, [and] politics, than we possess today.'

Richard Helms, former DCI, 1983

Previous chapters have described the complexity of a sophisticated intelligence chain and the tools, methods, problems and limitations of the collectors. This chapter is focused on the segment of the chain that has the responsibility for analysing, interpreting and finally creating an intelligence mosaic from the raw intelligence, in order to present a conclusion to the customers and consumers of intelligence. In Britain this process is called the assessment process; in the US 'estimates'. The process is an essential part of the intelligence chain.

Unlike the collectors with their spies and gadgets, the assessors work behind the scenes, and their essential, and usually admirable, performance has had no public chronicler in fiction or otherwise. There have been no famous novels about intelligence assessors; no Joseph Conrad,

Compton Mackenzie, Graham Greene, Ian Fleming or John le Carré, to mock, romanticise or discuss the machinery of assessment. Nor in the event of intelligence 'failure' does the dry subject of the assessment machinery receive much coverage. We only hear of the assessment process obliquely on some rare occasion, such as the unprecedented use of the JIC to produce a public assessment in late 2002 in the context of the vexed question as to whether Iraq had WMD.

But even in the retrospective scrutiny of the Iraqi WMD case the subject of the machinery of assessment was hardly touched upon. The issues of interest to the media were not the organisation and bureaucratic habits of the British intelligence machinery, but the personalities of individual performers whose heads were above the parapet. And, as in the Falkland Islands Review into 'the way in which the responsibilities of Government in relation to the … Islands and their Dependencies were discharged in the period leading up to the Argentine invasion of the … Islands on 2 April 1982', the inquiries into the WMD affair stuck very strictly to their terms of reference and gave us little enlightenment on the bureaucratic tangle that contributed to the unfortunate results. Boring as the subject may seem in comparison with the more glamorous profession of collecting intelligence, good assessment is key to good intelligence and should, perhaps, be given more attention.

The British Government seems to find it as difficult as the British public to take much interest in this recondite subject. The major shake up of the national machinery, undertaken by the leadership of Sir Burke Trend, Cabinet Secretary, in 1968 provided Britain for the first time in history with an intelligence staff to support the work of the JIC. Previously the JIC had no Assessment Staff; all the assessment work was done in departments or agencies, and the JIC Secretariat, which was only big enough to cobble it together and keep the paper flowing, had no capacity for research.

The new Assessment Staff establishment, which was about twenty strong, was composed of officials on secondment and sat alongside the Secretariat and the newly appointed Intelligence Coordinator. My appointment as Secretary of the JIC coincided with the beginning of the new dispensation. The Current Intelligence Groups, each of which dealt with a particular area of the world, produced an impressive volume of useful assessment using all sources available to them. Their reports were scrutinised and perhaps modified before being issued as JIC documents.

This model was an improvement on the previous system but no long-term solution had been found to provide permanent staff. The executive staff were permanent civil servants who did a magnificent job in keeping the machine running smoothly. But the Secretariat and Assessment Staff and, indeed, the Committee members themselves, were all birds of passage with a career to attend to outside the Cabinet Office, and few were likely to serve for even three years. And, not to put too fine a point on it, there was not one who had any credentials as an experienced assessment officer. From the Coordinator downwards, we had all earned our spurs elsewhere.

In the US however, by 1968, the profession of intelligence assessor was a well-recognised alternative to a career in academia or business. As an analyst, Robert Gates rose from a junior rank on the research side of the CIA to become Deputy Director of Central Intelligence, then to Director of Central Intelligence and, finally, Secretary of Defence. It is difficult to believe that an assessor could aspire to analogous heights in the UK.

The price Britain has paid is unquantifiable, but it certainly includes the damage done by the constant reinvention of the intelligence wheel by people who have not done their homework on intelligence history. For example, Trend's 1968 reform of the JIC included recommendations about creating an assessments cadre. In 2004 the Butler Review into intelligence on Iraq's alleged WMD capability noted the same point. The recommendation had not been implemented and assessors were left to learn on the job using their wits.

The beginning of the First World War is a good example of the dire consequences that can arise from wrong assessment. It was a worldwide conflagration on a scale never before experienced, or imagined, except in science fiction. In 1914 there was plenty of good intelligence available to all the major players, Sigint was already a powerful intelligence weapon and the crowned heads of the European states were all closely related. They talked of cousin Willie, the Kaiser, and Nicky, the Tsar, wrote soothing letters to each other and assumed that common sense would prevail. It was unthinkable that the Great Powers could be propelled inexorably to a gigantic, unwanted, world war. The leaders in Europe did not conceive of such a catastrophe until the troop trains began to move hundreds of thousands of combatants.

Professor Geoffrey Blainey, the Australian historian, in his masterly book *The Causes of War* suggests many reasons why intelligence communities fail to foresee the dangers ahead.[1] For example, he points to the Japanese attacks on the Russian naval base at Port Arthur in 1904 and on the US naval base at Pearl Harbor in 1941. The parallels are remarkable. In both cases the Japanese capacity for war, skill and daring, were underestimated; in both cases the garrisons' fleet was successfully attacked by Japanese torpedoes, and both Russia and the US were caught napping.

On both occasions it was well known that serious tension was growing and that the Japanese were in a belligerent mood, so there was no excuse for not being on the alert. The Russian and US garrison commanders were content with their appreciation that their bases were impregnable, and anyway Japan was too far away. Neither Russian nor US intelligence had predicted the time, place or method of attack, but the main failure was the obstinate complacency of the customers; the policymakers and the operational commanders ignored the warning signals and, as a result, failed to feel a sense of urgency. Complacency, arrogance, racial bias and mirror imaging all had their part to play, and allowed the Japanese twice in forty years to make a first, devastating attack on fortresses, which their Western enemies smugly believed to be impregnable.

Discovering the number of tanks, aircraft, and so on in the enemy forces has become ever easier with the development of satellite photography, drones and infrared detection. Intentions, however, are difficult to discover. Terrorists' overall intentions are declared from the house tops, whether it is independence or jihad. Their operational plans, however, are much harder to ascertain, as the 9/11 attacks highlighted. It was not the first hijacking of a commercial airliner, but there had never been a case of terrorists using an aircraft as a flying fire bomb. Thousands of officers, people, and every form of technical aid, produced a mass of information but only human imagination, not computers, could predict such an unprecedented attack, which had, however, been portrayed in a popular Tom Clancy novel.[2]

As I write the world faces the Russian leader, Vladimir Putin, trained in the KGB, his overriding object to grasp power and recover the Russian Empire. His annexation of Crimea should have been interpreted as a warning shot, but in a world which prefers optimism to pessimism, it has been largely ignored. Putin has been displaying his true colours for a long time. It is not clear why the Western world has been so surprised to find that their erstwhile strategic ally was not a friend, but probably an enemy.

Intelligence services, even if they have managed to purloin a valid copy of the latest Politburo minutes, can do no more than enlighten their customers on what the target has allowed to be put in his or her mouth. There is no guarantee that, even if the record is correct, they will not change their minds. Intentions are not merely secrets, they are mysteries, and intelligence on them will continue to be a matter of guesswork, never certainty.

The remainder of this chapter addresses the common fallacies which mar intelligence assessment: mirror imaging, groupthink, over-reliance on numbers, wishful thinking and assuming the grass is greener on the other side. The chapter's headings are not based on any scholarly or official tome on intelligence methods. Like the terms used in the previous chapter, some will be familiar to the general reader and some will not. Fundamentally, we are looking at common fallacies that have been responsible throughout the ages for dangerously wrong appreciations and woefully wrong predictions about enemy intentions. The central theme of the chapter is the importance of quality assessment.

Mirror Imaging

This is a subject of huge importance and a cause of many errors. Mirror imaging is the mistake of forgetting that not everyone thinks as we do. It is a trap for all. Understanding the mind of another person, even a person brought up in the same society, is no easy matter. It is very much more difficult to understand and anticipate the thought processes of people from a different culture, and our assessment is likely to be wrong if we assume that the target shares our views and prejudices. Among mirror imaging's latest manifestations is the belief held by some in the West that the people of Iraq and Afghanistan share our priorities and values. If, as all too frequently happens, an intelligence community falls into the trap of mirror imaging, a nation may suffer great harm.

The mirror imaging fallacy can lead to entirely false assumptions; thus:

> We vastly out number the enemy;
> We would not dream of attacking against such odds;
> Therefore the enemy will not attack.

It is dangerous whether in peace or war to take it for granted that all have the same priorities and perceptions, and use the same moral compass. In the military field, for example, people have made many wrong assessments that the enemy will react as they themselves would in any given circumstances; that the enemy will be making military appreciations on the same basis as the home team. But the enemy may not share your views on the value of human life, or may not have an accurate picture of the strength of the defence and, therefore, will not be aware of the high casualty rate they must face. They may also have different views on the ratio of troops required for success, or on the degree of support from artillery, tanks and aircraft that your own planners judge are necessary to guarantee success.

In Vietnam, the failure to understand the differences between the cultures of the opposing forces led to fatal underestimations of the fighting potential of the far less well equipped North Vietnamese forces. At Dien Bien Phu the French planners totally failed to anticipate the ability of an underdeveloped nation to succeed militarily in a situation that would have looked impossible to a Western commander. The mistake would, perhaps, not have been made had the French remembered that two thousand years before, Romans, Greeks, Egyptians, and many others, had been able to produce vast structures using nothing except manpower.

There is another aspect of mirror imaging which affects both civil and military attempts to estimate intentions, that most difficult of intelligence targets. You do not know the exact content of the target's database, and it is unlikely that it is exactly the same as yours. Nor can you be certain that the enemy's interpretation is the same as yours. There are many examples of major differences of interpretation of facts and intelligence made by the West and the Soviet Union during the Second World War, each because of very different cultures and histories.

Consider the case of the KGB, who were exploiting their wartime opportunities to the full to spy on their Western allies. They refused to believe that we were not behaving in a similar fashion. So when Philby and the other members of the Soviet espionage ring, 'the Cambridge Five', reported that there were no British clandestine operations inside the Soviet Union, the KGB interpreted this as evidence that Philby and company were double agents, and that they were reporting lies and deceptions. The KGB continued throughout the war to mistrust Philby's reporting.

However, it is not easy to find staff with a good understanding of another culture. A thorough understanding of the differences between our society and that of the target country is unlikely to be acquired by academic study alone. But since it is clearly a counsel of impossible perfection to suggest that every neophyte assessor can have the opportunity to live and work in the society in which they are to specialise, we can only hope to burn into the minds of the trainees the need to remember that people do not all react or think in the same way. They should also be encouraged to have the humility to accept that they can only partially understand the mindsets of people from a different background.

People used to remark in Malaya and China, 'it's so easy for you, you speak the language.' Although that facilitated an understanding of what pleased and annoyed them, language skills alone were not the central basis for success; it was working with them daily that had brought about some degree of understanding. Airport bookshops of the world are well stocked with books claiming to inform the business traveller 'how to do business in country X'. They remind the reader that they are about to enter an arena where significant differences because of culture and custom may cause serious difficulties, embarrassment and animosity. The two sides may have very different concepts of time scales, business ethics, bribery, the sanctity of contracts and so on.

Intelligence officers ought to be given training on this aspect of life. It should not be assumed that, having recruited bright and able graduates with excellent degrees, they can be relied upon to educate themselves so that they do not fall into the mirror imaging trap. The British Imperial Services, who were paid for by local governments across the empire, took the view that, however high the quality of their recruits they should be required to serve an apprenticeship of four years as cadets, during which time they had to study the language, law, history and culture of their territory. Those who failed their examination were not confirmed in their appointments.

There have been many occasions when Britons with first-class degrees were badly wrong in their conclusions because of mirror imaging. One example was provided by the assessment of Soviet intentions after the Prague Spring of 1968. The intelligence picture was clear: the Soviet forces deployed in preparation for their annual manoeuvres, along the Czech border, were considerably larger than usual, and there were more than enough to invade and subdue their Czech satellite. The question which neither photography nor Sigint could answer, and which no agent had answered either, was whether the Soviets would invade. The Chairman of the committee concerned, a generalist who had the highest intellectual qualifications, overruled the views of the specialists round the table and insisted that the Soviets would not invade because of the adverse effect such an act would have on world opinion. The Soviets, however, were much less concerned with world opinion than they were with the fact that the Prague Spring had set a dangerous precedent that gave encouragement to dissidents and reformers among the Soviet satellites, and thus endangered the Soviet sphere of influence. The Soviet leaders did not give a kopek for world opinion.

Another example of flawed assessment due to mirror imaging was provided by China in 1989. For a month, ever growing crowds of Chinese thronged Changan Da Jie, the central boulevard of Beijing, supporting the students who were camped in Tian Anmen, a vast central square. The Chinese Government became increasingly infuriated by the sight of protesters bearing banners demanding freedom, the end of corruption and nepotism and so on, even mocking the patriarch Deng Xiaoping as 'Little Bottle'. The capital of China came to a standstill and there was a great loss of face. The Western media was giving maximum coverage to the situation, praising the outbreak of democratic fervour.

It was indeed impressive, but it was also unrealistic to suppose that the Politburo would allow the protests to continue. Their priority was to restore order and not to please world opinion. So the demonstrators were crushed violently by the Army, as the Imperial Cossack Cavalry had crushed demonstrations in Moscow at the beginning of the century, when the Russians attempted to appeal to the Tsar, their 'Little Father'.

The tragic carnage in Beijing appeared to take the West by surprise. But I was in Beijing at the time and I found it difficult to see any ending other than brutal suppression. There were many reasons for this assessment. Authoritarian regimes, be they Russian, Chinese or North Korean, Communist or Fascist, do not develop traditions of peaceful handling of riots and civil commotions; they have no doctrine of minimum force, or trained riot squads. It seemed naïve to expect the Chinese Government, enraged by the disrespectful attitude of the student leaders, and incensed by the worldwide coverage of the chaos in Beijing, to show moderation. It ended with a bloody show of force. The West would not have been surprised had they not been prone to mirror imaging. They assumed wrongly that the Chinese Government would give the same weight as the western democracies did to world opinion, and to concepts such as the rule of law and human rights. For the Chinese

Government such things were subsidiary to the restoration of order and of 'face'.

Mirror imaging is as significant a cause of mis-assessment as any form of fallacious thinking. If the assessors are highly educated Western liberals, they will need to be particularly conscious of the dangers inherent in assuming that the foreigner has the same views on ethics, law and so on. Like the rest of the pitfalls discussed here, mirror imaging is not the prerogative of intelligence assessors alone; it is part of general life. As the old saying has it, 'there's nowt so queer as folk', and getting fully into the mind of another person is no easy task. The task is infinitely more difficult if one is trying to get into the mind of someone from a totally different culture and with different priorities and prejudices. Further, an adequate understanding is more likely to be acquired after some time working and living in the country concerned through a sort of osmosis than by reading alone. Although it is obviously impossible to offer to every fledgling assessor a long apprenticeship in the field, it is clearly of great importance that somehow the dangers of mirror imaging are burnt into their minds.

Groupthink

This is a common cause of mistaken opinion and mistaken assessment. It is convenient to join the mob and agree with their view; it takes energy and courage to take an independent line. Groupthink means the received wisdom: the authorised view of an institution, bureaucracy or military organisation. It is a damaging form of thought. The 1973 Yom Kippur war illustrates the principle. In this example the blanket of complacency led to the acceptance of the most comfortable thesis. The Egyptians were holding another annual military exercise, scurrying around the Middle East in a way that suggested panic rather than confidence. In late September a courageous, independent minded Israeli intelligence officer decided that the enemy activity was not merely another defensive exercise, but suggested something much more aggressive. He submitted his report to higher command, who suppressed it. On 6 October the attack commenced and the Israelis were caught by surprise. Groupthink does not welcome challenges, particularly if they come from junior officers.

The Numbers Fallacy

The numbers fallacy, like the others described in this chapter, is not the monopoly of the intelligence community. It also exists in the business world, for example, where accountants are sometimes guilty of thinking that money is everything and business people ignore the experiments that have shown that job satisfaction, loyalty and other non-financial factors are important too.

There are many examples from the Second World War of numbers being a poor guide. The overwhelming numbers of Soviet troops, tanks and aircraft did not give them an easy victory over German forces. In 1941 the Soviets had six times more tanks and five times more aircraft than the invading Germans. Yet the Germans walked all over the Soviets because they were better trained, better led and their equipment was of higher quality.

While overestimating the strength of the enemy should be avoided, so too should the habit of counting armoured fighting vehicles in order to determine a threat. Quality, ease of maintenance, fuel requirements, crew conditions, training, speed, endurance, effectiveness of armour and firing systems, and other exotica must also be considered. And even if military hardware, personnel and weapons are equal, other imponderables such as leadership, morale, imagination, tactics, and command and control will affect the outcome of an engagement. Although quality must be considered when assessing an enemy's strengths, it is very difficult to measure. And however good the weapon, the performance of the user may prove decisive.

The Cold War provided many examples of the uncritical use of numbers to assess enemy threats and strength. Both West and East were guilty of confusing quantity with quality; both issued alarmist accounts of the opponents' capabilities and possible intentions. The military establishments naturally found it convenient when seeking increased budgets to talk of numbers without discussion of quality. The Soviet military was large and the prospect of a swarm of tanks and aircraft, and hordes of soldiers invading Western Europe, backed by missiles, was indeed alarming. But did the quality match the quantity? Somehow the assessors were so mesmerised by the numbers that they barely considered other factors. It was a curious general failure. It was, as the scientists used to say, comparing apples with oranges. The quality of the Soviet conscripts, almost two million per year, drafted for a two-year stint of

National Service, should have been given more attention. Comparisons of air strength based on numbers alone were also misleading: for example the West had an overwhelming advantage in the amount of training time given to pilots. Further, attempts to arrive at solid conclusions by comparing budgets was a singularly useless, disingenuous or even mendacious, exercise. All defence budgets are opaque and the doubling of a budget does not guarantee a doubling of production. There never was a reliable measure of productivity.

A useful overview of the nature and extent of military exaggerations during the Cold War is provided in a book by someone, who like me, went to Glenalmond College and Worcester College Oxford, and appears to have been infected, like me, with an instinct to challenge the received wisdom. Andrew Cockburn's *The Threat* gives an excellent picture of how the military machines of the US and the Soviet Union went about the task of persuading their governments of the need for vast expenditure on defence by emphasising numbers.[3]

The missile gap of the late 1950s and early 1960s, a period when US intelligence produced inaccurate assessments of Soviet missile production and which chilled the blood of the West, was another area where comparing numbers was particularly unhelpful. The world had no experience of Intercontinental Ballistic Missiles (ICBMs) in battle, so the experts had only theoretical data upon which to base their assessments. They had been tested over comparatively short ranges. We do know that there were many failures in the test firings. These ICBMs were unreliable. The smaller rocket systems tested also illustrated the gap between theory and practice. In the Yom Kippur War of 1973, the Israelis claimed that only one of their aircraft was hit for every 100 SAM-6 (Surface to Air Missiles) that were fired. The hand-held SAM-7 was much less effective: 5,000 hand-held SAM-7s were launched but with only two confirmed, and four possible, kills. Remember too that the US made a gallant effort to assess the state of the Vietnam War on the basis of numbers. Their charts produced proved useless.

The numbers fallacy remains just as much a danger today. Governments continue to make efforts to assign numbers to terrorists and their supporters, insurgent groups who threaten stability in the Middle East, and Russian forces in and near Ukraine. In 2014 the CIA was forced to triple its estimate of the number of Islamic State fighters in Iraq and Syria in the light of a review of recent intelligence reports, demonstrating just how difficult it is to produce accurate estimates of this kind. Numbers still inform policy and military decisions about how to tackle these threats. But assessors must remain wary of the dangers of placing too much confidence in numbers, and of underemphasising the importance of qualitative factors.

Wishful Thinking

Everyone has, at some time, fallen into the trap of mixing hope with reality. In a perfect world wishes must be followed by hard-headed assessment. Case officers and assessors need to be on guard against the over-optimism of agents, particularly those who are not themselves going to be personally involved in action.

The ancient case of the Trojan horse provides a fine example of the dangerous influence of wishful thinking. The Trojans awoke one morning to find that the Greek forces, which had been besieging them, had sailed away leaving a large wooden horse outside the main gate. Cassandra, the local soothsayer, was a lone pessimistic voice crying 'wolf'. The Trojan leaders however, weary with war, preferred an optimistic assessment that the Greeks had given up their plan to capture Troy and sailed away for good leaving behind the horse as a gesture of goodwill. Acting on this wishful thinking, the Trojan leaders gave orders to enlarge the main gateway so that the wooden horse could be dragged inside the city walls. In the middle of the night the belly of the horse opened and special Greek forces crept out to take over the city. The Greek *coup de main* is one of many examples when someone crying 'wolf' has been right.

Before Pearl Harbor, the chief intelligence officer at the US base, Captain Laycock, repeatedly warned that the Japanese were in a belligerent mood and likely to go to war. His colleagues, who were engaged in wishful thinking, laughed at him, but he was later proved right.

The prelude to President Galtieri's 1982 invasion of the Falklands provides a further example of the prevalence of wishful thinking. In the 1970s the Argentinians had come near to war. Prime Minister James Callaghan used SIS to pass a gentle warning to them that we had nuclear submarines in the area and would use them if they went to war.[4] The warning, passed discreetly via intelligence channels, had the desired effect, and the Argentinians backed off. The belligerent new President

Galtieri came to power in 1981 promising that he would not put up with further British prevarications and procrastinations, and would recover the Falklands. The British Government had no need of secret intelligence to alert them to the danger to the Falklands, but since no viable defence plan for the territory would be affordable in peacetime, their policy was 'to hope for the best'. In fact, Galtieri's decision to invade was logical and there was no excuse for surprise. Wishful thinking, complacency, and no doubt Foreign Office assertions that their negotiations with the Argentinians would, as they had in the past, prove successful all played their part in Britain's flawed expectation that there would be no attack.

The Grass is Greener

The problems created by complacency, false confidence and groupthink have already been noted. None of the faults encountered are specifically endemic to the intelligence industry, they are commonplace in every walk of life, although it is easier to identify such failings after disaster has struck in the context of some major investigation than in everyday life. Another bad habit to which the military in particular are prone is the idea that the grass is always greener on the other pasture, and that, therefore, the enemy has the better weapons and equipment.

I first met this syndrome during the Second World War when I commanded an Infantry Anti-Tank Platoon in Normandy. We had been provided with six 6-pounder guns, handed on from the Royal Artillery who had been issued with 17-pounders. The British gunners did not conceal their belief that we had been handed useless peashooters, which were no match for modern German tanks, sporting five-inch thick plates of frontal steel. I listened politely to the comments of the experts newly returned from their battles in the desert and hoped that training and tactics would help us since we did not intend to take the Panzers head on, but shoot diagonally at the flank and rear of the attacking tanks, where the armour was thinner.

On 1 July 1944 we had the opportunity to put our training and tactics to the test in a daylong battle against strong German Panzer attacks. By the end of the day my guns were credited with twelve kills: not bad for peashooters. I had three months in hospital to brood on the discrepancy between the pessimistic judgements of the experts and the reality, but it was another forty years before, while involved in writing a book about the battle, I discovered the range tables, which presumably caused the experts to declare that our rounds would bounce off German armour. The tables showed that at its maximum range the 6-pounder would not penetrate the frontal armour of a Tiger tank. We, however, had been fighting at close quarters and were not shooting at the frontal armour, so the range tables had little relevance.

Conclusion

The assessor is faced with many potential pitfalls, as explained in this chapter. They must strive for objectivity when interpreting the intelligence available to them. Achieving objectivity is not easy, as our analyses of what we see, hear and read are influenced by our own views. Being aware of how errors can creep in to assessment is an important step towards avoiding these errors.

Intelligence deals not only with facts but with attempts to fathom the mental state of human beings. This is difficult enough to do in public polling exercises; it is infinitely more difficult when guesswork, not a poll, is the basis for an assessment. The human mind is a mystery and minds may change overnight. The biggest challenge of all may be to persuade the customer of the wickedness of the outside world, and that foreigners are not necessarily thirsting for democracy and all the trappings of a modern state. Perhaps, however, we can forgive busy politicians for failing to find time in their gruelling schedules to read enough history to understand that not everyone has the same view of right and wrong. But there is less excuse for intelligence officers, and the intelligence community must try hard not to fall into such common traps as those listed above.

It is important that we recognise the debt we owe to the unsung heroes and heroines who devote their lives to working in the intelligence engine room. Without them the most brilliant Humint or Techint would be of little use. We must strive to provide a career structure for people prepared to devote their lives to the art of assessment. We should also remember the need for country specialisation at a time when the Foreign and Commonwealth Office has downplayed the importance of area specialisations for which, in imperial days, the British were renowned. The intelligence community must fill the gap once filled by the Imperial Services, colonial and consular.

7

MORAL DILEMMAS

'Gentlemen do not read each other's mail.'

Henry Stimson, US Secretary of State, 1929

'When the fate of a nation and the lives of its soldiers are at stake, gentlemen do read each other's mail—if they can get their hands on it.'

Allen Dulles, former DCI, 1963

'As motives [for spying] ideological and patriotic convictions stand at the top of the list.'

Allen Dulles, former DCI, 1963

'The only justification a soldier or a spy can have is the moral worth of the cause he represents.'

William Hood, formerly CIA, 1993

'When they feel threatened they want a lot of it [intelligence], and when they don't, they tend to regard the whole thing as somewhat immoral.'

Vernon Walters, former DDCI, 1978

'You have to be a bit of a villain for that sort of work.'

William Skardon, renowned MI5 interrogator, in an interview with author Philip Knightley, 1967

'Two presidents, when I was Director, told me in almost identical words, "Okay, but don't get caught."'

Richard Helms, former DCI, 1996

'The gathering of knowledge by clandestine means was repulsive to the feelings of English Gentlemen.'

Official British History of the Crimean War

Let us first dispose of the cynics' easy jibe about oxymorons and intelligence ethics. Soldiers are trained to kill, intelligence people trained to spy and as long as the military and intelligence people carry out their tasks on behalf of their nation, under the rules laid down by their government, they are not criminals but servants of the state. An instructor in an intelligence school might wake his class up by saying, 'you have been hired by the Crown to spy and it is my job to see that you are efficient spies' and assume that all the recruits were comfortable with the idea that activities which would normally be considered immoral disreputable or criminal were condoned if carried out on duty.

This chapter's discussion of moral dilemmas is positioned alongside the other chapters on the machinery and methodology of intelligence because the quandaries it presents can be found in a diverse range of intelligence activities. There are, for example, tensions between secrecy and the oversight of intelligence, questions over whether blackmail should be used to obtain intelligence, and moral dilemmas raised by the use of torture in connection with efforts to collect intelligence by interrogation. The intelligence community and the consumers of intelligence face a range of ethical challenges and moral dilemmas as well as the practical challenges discussed earlier in this book.

Torture and Interrogation

When those interested in intelligence gather together at conferences to talk about ethics, the subject most likely to be discussed is the collection of intelligence by interrogation, although interrogation is not a direct concern for most intelligence officers. A case officer is not in the business of bullying or torturing their sources. Their task is to recruit and befriend agents, building a close relationship based on trust, mutual understanding, shared values and interests. A successful Humint case is likely to be one where there is a mutually beneficial partnership. Such a relationship bears no resemblance to the sometimes adversarial relationship between an interrogator and a suspect, where one party is trying to extract information and the other may be trying to conceal the truth.

The best interrogators, it is said, are born, not made. They need intelligence, patience, a good memory, and the skills of a psychologist. Some interrogators have been successful because of dogged determination, wearing suspects down through days and nights of gentle but insistent questioning until the victims are so bored that they collaborate in order to bring the agony to an end. Good interrogators are endowed with capacious memories, quick intelligence, and the qualities of a successful barrister. Interrogators can also be brilliant communicators who somehow persuade the victim that they are both on the same side.

At a recent seminar on intelligence ethics, I found that there was no discussion of the occasional need for hostile interrogation. Those present seemed to be content to accept without question the European Convention on Human Rights and Fundamental Freedoms' prohibition of torture and other forms of ill-treatment. No-one remarked that Western fastidiousness provided terrorist instructors with a useful training tool: since Western interrogators were forbidden to exert 'pressure', the prisoners only had to maintain denials or silence in order to win.

There is a need for discussion about definitions of terms. The ancient Chinese and Greek philosophers understood full well that unless we defined our terms, debate was meaningless. In 1540 an English dictionary defined torture as 'the infliction of excruciating pain or suffering in order to force an unwilling witness to give information'. This definition is echoed in the UN Convention Against Torture and Other Cruel, Inhuman or Degrading Treatment or Punishment, signed by the UK on 15 March 1985. In the Convention's definition, torture 'means any act by which severe pain or suffering, whether physical or mental, is intentionally inflicted on a person for such purposes as obtaining from him or a third person information or a confession'.

Those responsible for drawing up the UN rules and definitions were guilty of mirror imaging. Their reactions to controversial techniques would probably be different to those from other cultures and, perhaps, harsher environments. A sophisticated Western jurist or judge brought up in comfortable civilised circumstances is unlikely to have the same reactions to the 'controversial' techniques as someone brought up in a society with a harsher culture. What for one person is torture or degrading treatment may for another be mere discomfort. Reaction to pressure—a term distinct from torture—is very individual. And whether the victim succumbs depends on many different factors, such as self-esteem, will, conscience, and loyalty to colleagues or cause. These are matters likely to differ dramatically according to character, personality, hardiness, background and training.

Our general revulsion against torture is of comparatively recent date. In 1640 England led the way by abolishing torture and by 1789 the French followed suit, but Europe was accustomed to barbaric actions, including public executions, beheadings, burning at the stake, and hanging, drawing and quartering. Most people today are opposed to the use of instruments of physical torture such as the mediaeval rack and thumbscrew, the twentieth century cattle prod or water torture: but some continue to practise beheadings, execution by stoning and public floggings.

The debate on interrogation has tended to be a *dialogue des sourds*: minds made up already. The spectrum of views on interrogation in the West falls into three parts. At one extreme are the ethical absolutists who renounce any form of pressure to extract statements from prisoners, arguing that this is an abuse of human rights. Somewhere in the middle are those who emphasise that intelligence extracted as a result of pressure is unreliable, since the prisoners may tell lies in order to earn their freedom. Therefore on practical grounds, pressure should be banned. Sir Dick White took the view that an interrogator only needed intellectual skills. But I noted that when MI5 faced Philby their intellectual skills did not persuade him to confess. The third group consists of those who say they have learnt by experience that well trained 'hard' individuals seldom succumb to kind words, cups of tea or intellectual dominance.

Historical examples

Not everyone agrees that no pressure should be used to tip the balance in the interrogator's favour. Many civilian and military lives were saved as a result of the tactics employed in Malaya in the 1950s. Uncooperative prisoners did not enjoy home comforts: temperatures could be unpleasant, food was basic and sleep was disturbed. We were advocates of the 'ticking bomb' justification: the prisoner's rights were not superior to those of potential victims who might be tortured in front of their despairing families before being brutally murdered. This is delicate ground indeed: one person's discomfort may seem torture to a gently reared judge.

I was never formally part of the interrogation process in Malaya although I was involved in the discussions about rewards and incentives in the general context of our psywar programme, and I was present during some interrogations, acting as a Chinese-speaking interpreter for SB.[1] There was no hint of torture in interrogations that I attended. CTs who had surrendered or been captured were faced with a simple choice: collaborate and be rewarded with generous cash rewards and even with freedom, or refuse and face the prospect of lengthy imprisonment and possibly execution.

Fortunately few of our captured CTs had strong ideological convictions. The surrendered enemy personnel had already decided that they had backed the wrong horse and many captured enemy personnel were already disillusioned and ripe for defection. Some of the senior cadres were little more than gangsters who had decided that the Malayan Communist Party was a promising form of secret society in which they could expect to enjoy greater privileges than they had previously enjoyed as a Triad officer. There were few died-in-the-wool fanatical Communists.

We found that for the most part friendliness and generous treatment, coupled with promises of early freedom and rehabilitation, worked well. Usually there was a rapid turning of the coat and collaboration; some went to work immediately acting as guides to jungle squads seeking terrorist camps. We were also aided by excellent Chinese supporting staff who could tie the prisoners in knots on ideology. They knew a great deal more about Marxist Leninism and Mao's doctrines than most of the Malayan Communists.

A rare record of practical experience is provided by Camp 020. MI5 opened this facility in July 1940. They had turned Latchmere, a former military hospital, into an efficient interrogation centre equipped with plenty of hidden microphones. Between 1940 and 1945, 480 interrogation cases were handled there. The Commandant was Lieutenant-Colonel Robin Stephens, who was a stern character in the mould of some gruff, bulldog hero of *Boy's Own Paper*. Stephens did not like 'Huns' and made no secret of the low opinion he held of the foreign spies who passed through the camp. In one of his reports he remarks that, '[t]he majority of the spies were as treacherous a gang as could be found in the universe.' These were all comparatively low-grade agents, recruited casually by the Germans and given relatively easy tasks. Most were spying for money.

To staff and prisoners alike Stephens gave the impression of a fierce, single minded officer to be obeyed. He insisted that a good interrogator must hate the enemy. His teams usually succeeded in 'breaking' the prisoners, although in one case it took seventy-seven days. The process always began with the prisoner dressed in ill-fitting civilian clothes marked by a large triangular white patch, standing to attention. The interrogators made it clear that they knew enough about the prisoner already to convict them and all that was required was a full confession, and if he or she collaborated it might be possible to arrange that they would not be executed.

In peacetime these proceedings might have been derailed by a defence barrister. But this was wartime. Britain was the only European country which had not succumbed to the Nazi hordes. If you had been found in possession of equipment which could have no other purpose than clandestine activity, conviction was almost certain. The penalty for espionage could be death.

As the Allies advanced through Europe, Stephens, now a Colonel, took command in Forward Interrogation Centres, and was accused of torture and abuse. Stephens' charges included insufficient clothing, cold water thrown into cells in winter, scrubbing out by prisoners, insufficient medical attention, bullying and harassment by guards, and solitary confinement as a punishment for not answering questions. Stephens was acquitted at a court martial. He had always forbidden physical violence, but demanded strict discipline and determined, unremitting, interrogation. His doctrine included that:

Figuratively, a spy in war should be held at the point of a bayonet.
Violence is taboo ... [because] it lowers the standard of information.
Pressure is attained by personality, tone, and rapidity of question; insistence upon an immediate answer, recapitulation.
Never promise, never bargain. The man's neck is in your grasp.
Blow hot, blow cold. No respite, no time to recover, no time to plan.[2]

Sometimes interrogations went on all night, exhausting interrogators and prisoners alike. In the particular circumstances that Stephens was confronted with, these methods appear to have been successful. It is important to remember, though, that what is effective, and what is appropriate, depends upon many factors, including whether it is wartime or peacetime, and the background and nature of the people being interrogated.

Two further historical examples are useful here. They confirm that results can vary enormously according to the character of the prisoner. The first is the case of a CIA officer whose job was to glean intelligence that might help to reduce the damage from rocket attacks on Saigon. His colleagues in Vietnamese military intelligence believed in torture, but their barbarities produced nothing of value. The CIA officer persuaded his Vietnamese colleagues to hand over the battered Vietcong prisoner who had refused to talk. The CIA officer tended his wounds, fed him well, let him meet his family and showed him the sights of a prosperous, vibrant Saigon. The prisoner decided to collaborate and produced actionable intelligence, which helped the defence against Vietcong rocket attacks. The moral is obvious: kindness can pay.

The second story is of Nien Cheng, the widow of a pre-revolution Chinese diplomat who was part of the tiny coterie of Chinese in Shanghai who were prepared to stay in touch with foreigners. Nien was a sophisticated well-travelled graduate of London University who when she visited Britain usually stayed with the Duchess of Gloucester. She was arrested when the Cultural Revolution began, condemned to solitary confinement and tormented for five years, stoutly refusing to sign a confession. Nien kept up her fighting spirit, partly furious against the evil regime that had taken over her beloved country and partly determined to see her daughter again. The European Court of Human Rights in Strasbourg would certainly have found that her treatment was cruel, degrading and inhuman. She was slapped, beaten, kicked, bounced against the wall, and for a long period her hands were so tightly handcuffed behind her back so that her hands and arms swelled horribly. Her cell was freezing in winter and unpleasantly hot in summer; her rations consisted of watery soup and boiled rice. Medical treatment was refused for her increasing number of ailments, which included haemorrhaging, bleeding gums, swollen joints and open wounds. Her interrogators assumed that like most detainees Nien would eventually decide to make a confession in order to escape the miseries of her cell. They were wrong: she left the prison bloody but unbowed. Nien is a reminder that resistance is not necessarily dependent on fitness, training, age, health or fanaticism. She stood up to her torturers for moral reasons, and willpower prevailed over pain.[3]

America's views

The US, having moved during the twentieth century from Secretary Stimson's high-minded position of 'gentlemen do not read each other's mail' to the creation of the largest intelligence community in the democratic world, is not in step with Europe. CIA documents available on the internet appearing under the name KUBARK (the cryptonym for CIA Headquarters) attempt to bring together, in language understandable by the layperson, the findings of psychologists on human reaction to pressure.[4]

The 1963 document warns that '[i]nterrogations conducted under compulsion or duress are especially likely to involve illegality ... [and] prior Headquarters approval ... must be obtained for the interrogation of any source ... if bodily harm is to be inflicted [or] [i]f medical, chemical, or electrical methods are to be used'. A less heavily redacted version, declassified in 2014, reveals that if the detention of the suspect was 'locally illegal and traceable to KUBARK ... retroactive Headquarters approval may be promptly requested by priority cable.'[5] The general tenor of both these handbooks is that pressure of some sort will be necessary to make recalcitrant prisoners talk. Intellectual dominance and patience will not always be enough.

Interrogation is described as a team effort in these handbooks; a continuum, planned in advance, where an expert analytical team supports the interrogators, possibly role-playing as 'good cop' and 'bad cop'. The support team follows the interrogation from an adjacent room, armed with access to all the relevant data ready to keep the interrogators supplied with supplementary material. Concealed microphones and cameras linked to recorders are used so the interrogators do not need to take notes. Recommendations include purpose built interrogation rooms to eliminate distractions and induce a sense of isolation. Disorientation techniques such as varying the times and durations of interrogation are also recommended. They suggest that the threat of physical pain may produce cooperation.

The public debate about interrogation methods has been much wider in the US than in the UK. A review commissioned by the Intelligence Science Board in 2005 produced a 325-page report concluding that the methods used by the US intelligence community were unreliable and suggesting that a wider and more scientific approach was needed. It agreed, however, that the use of 'highly coercive' techniques might sometimes be required. It is important to balance this claim against the damage that revelations about the US' use of so-called enhanced interrogation techniques post-9/11 have done to the country's reputation.

Part of the confusion in the debate about interrogation and torture stems from a failure to differentiate between the mindset of a normal prisoner of war and that of a jihadi. German, Italian and Japanese prisoners held during the Second World War were not usually fanatics. Many wanted to live and cooperated accordingly. Jihadi terrorists, however, are often completely dedicated to the cause. We certainly need additional efforts to undo the brainwashing carried out by vocal extremists.

On 9 March 2008 President George W. Bush vetoed a Congressional attempt to put new limits on the techniques that could be used for interrogation. Those in favour of Congress's attempt repeated the familiar argument that there was no evidence that harsh interrogation procedures produced more useful intelligence than gentler methods. The President argued that, '[b]ecause the danger remains, we need to ensure our intelligence officials have all the tools they need to stop the terrorists.' He continued, '[w]e have no higher responsibility than stopping terrorist attacks. And this is no time for Congress to abandon practices that have a proven track record of keeping America safe.'

General Michael Hayden, former Director of the CIA (2006–9), is reported to have announced that the US Army Field Manual on interrogation is an adequate guidebook, and that harsh methods are unnecessary or even counterproductive. But Bush maintained that the CIA should not be bound by rules written for the guidance of soldiers in combat. In 2014 the debate was once again given new life, this time by the declassification of parts of the Senate Select Committee's 2012 study of the CIA's detention and interrogation programme.[6] The dilemma will not disappear; interrogation methods need a great deal more study.

Northern Ireland and Strasbourg

In December 1971 the Irish Government filed an application with the European Commission of Human Rights in Strasbourg. It included an allegation that Britain had, during the interrogation of suspected terrorists interned without trial in Northern Ireland, violated Article 3 of the European Convention on Human Rights, which prohibits torture and inhuman and degrading treatment of prisoners. Seven years later the

European Court of Human Rights announced that Britain had not been guilty of torture, but had been guilty of the inhuman and degrading treatment of prisoners.

As Secretary of the JIC and staff officer to Sir Dick White, the Intelligence Coordinator, when the furore about Northern Ireland broke out, I was closely involved in the debate. With years of experience of interrogation techniques in Malaya, it was difficult to empathise with those who felt so strongly that to put a sack over the head of a detainee was to inflict degrading and inhuman treatment. Our targets in Malaya, the CTs, were in the habit of cold-blooded murder, often after torturing their prisoners. The IRA too showed little mercy to their captives.

My involvement in what came to be known as 'the Strasbourg case' began when White appeared in my office one morning brandishing a newspaper which had a banner headline about torture in Northern Ireland. The controversy was dealt with in a very typical British fashion. The great and the good, judges, Privy Counsellors, intelligence and security knights, and generals were consulted.[7] White and I were at one on the subject of the immense importance of the intelligence gained by interrogation, and in the country of the blind we had something to offer.

I have refreshed my memory by re-reading documents I drafted in 1971 and 1972, and other official papers that are now available in The National Archives. From the beginning I had taken the view that there would continue to be a public outcry and we should clarify that the objective of wall standing, hooding and white noise was not to soften up the prisoners, but to ensure maximum security in the early stages of an operation. These techniques reduced, for prisoners and staff, the chances of identifying individuals involved, the place of interrogation, and the overhearing of conversations and recognition of voices. The Intelligence Coordinator's recommendations incorporated my view. The softening up effect the techniques had on these prisoners as they awaited interrogation was acknowledged, but this was not the purpose of their use.

The Intelligence Coordinator's note for Privy Councillor Lord Parker's 1971–2 inquiry into interrogation practices emphasised the need to bear in mind that the intelligence produced by interrogation had become the most important source of intelligence available to the security forces in Northern Ireland. The Government was, however, scared. Prime Minister Edward Heath, who had not long before complained to the Secretary of the Cabinet that the military, security and intelligence services were all wet and asked for a list of things we might secretly do to inhibit the IRA, banned all the controversial techniques, hoping that this would persuade the Irish Government to withdraw their application to Strasbourg. Perhaps if, as I had advised at the beginning, we had apologised for mistakes made in the heat of the moment, the Irish Government might have been mollified.

White's notes make robust points about the psychological environment of interrogation, which were at odds with his earlier emphasis to me on the efficacy of intellectual domination. He wrote that successful interrogation requires that prisoners be brought to realise that they have reached the end of their particular road, that their freedom is entirely within our control, and they are now entirely alone. Their former comrades could neither help them nor condemn them further, nor exact reprisals upon them (my notations on the draft challenged this last point). White continued:

It is for him [the prisoner] and him alone to decide whether it is best for him to cooperate with his interrogators ... The conviction of having reached the end of the road is all the more complete when the suspect reaches it through his own introspection during periods of isolation in his cell and by reading the signs of his defeat in the impersonal and disciplined demeanour and conduct of those who control and question him.

There were certain grim essentials in the business.

The Coordinator's Recommendations included that:

a) Interrogation should be supervised by a senior police officer; the role of military officers should be advisory only.
b) There should be substantial information on a detainee's involvement in terrorist activity before he is selected for protracted interrogation.
c) The use of permitted techniques should be subject to medical scrutiny and advice.
d) The three techniques of wall-standing, hooding and white noise should be used for control, discipline and security purposes.
e) Records should be kept on the use of the three techniques.
f) There should be immediate investigation into the possibility of providing better purpose-built interrogation centres, to reduce the need to use the three techniques.

An outcome of the various official inquiries prompted by the use of hooding and other techniques in Northern Ireland was the appearance in

The National Archives of a short report by the Ministry of Defence describing the results achieved by interrogation of detainees in Northern Ireland. Since the Report was the only one of many submitted to the Parker Committee which was cleared for the public records, it seems reasonable to assume that it slipped through the security net by mistake.[8]

The Report claimed that new, or confirmatory intelligence, was obtained about both wings of the IRA. This included forty sheets of ORBAT, the identification of hundreds of IRA personnel, future operational plans, logistical and operational arrangements, locations of arms caches, locations of safe houses, descriptions of means of communications, and description of supply routes for arms and explosives. The intelligence obtained was actionable and of immediate, as well as of long-term, value. It helped the security forces in various ways, including the mounting of successful search and arrest operations, which in turn led to further identifications and successes, such as the discovery of a large arms cache. This report seems to justify the infliction of pressure on the suspects, although, of course, the opposition can point out that we cannot be sure that the same results could have been achieved without pressure. The Ministry of Defence also had reason to exaggerate in this account of intelligence gained from this controversial interrogation operation.

During the Irish imbroglio, White continued to argue that pressure was not needed to produce results from interrogation, but I managed to persuade him that wall standing, bags on heads, and white sound could be justified on security grounds, that sleep deprivation for both suspect and interrogators was an inevitable part of the operational process, and that a diet of bread and water was a long way from torture. Frank Steele, an SIS officer serving in Northern Ireland, described the controversial techniques as damned stupid and immoral. But Steele had even less direct experience of interrogation than White.

In the European Court of Human Rights in Strasbourg, seventeen judges agreed that the techniques amounted not to torture but instead constituted degrading and inhuman treatment. Judge M. Zekia offered the common-sense rider that the criteria are subjective; there will be a difference between the reaction of a healthy young person and that of a sick or old person. Sir Gerald FitzMaurice, a British judge, took the view that the controversial techniques were not inhuman. Perhaps His Honour had, like me, been educated at a British boarding school.

The techniques complained of in the Strasbourg case may seem mild, or at least of a different sort, compared with the revolting and obscene cruelties inflicted routinely by interrogators in police states. Penkovsky's notes described in detail the cruelties carried out in the basement of the KGB premises in Moscow, where innocent Russians were pitilessly interrogated. He describes one cell where, if the prisoner refused to 'sing' appropriately, hungry rats were loosed through a series of pipes to attack the victim, while the interrogator screamed through a microphone, 'now will you confess, you scoundrel?' People confessed, the guards drove the rats out with powerful jets of water and the prisoner was hustled out ready for execution. It was, said Penkovsky, 'terrible'.[9]

It seems to me, forty years on, that there has been little progress or advance in the study of interrogation techniques and the results of interrogation, and of the most effective permissible means of persuading prisoners to disgorge their intelligence. The absolutists' argument, based on the sanctity of human rights, seem to drown out all debate on the need to distinguish between 'hard' and 'soft' individuals.

Polygraphs and Lie Detectors

The polygraph method of interrogation deserves mention. It is popularly known as a lie detector, but also by more scientific names such as the measuring of electro-dermal responses or the systolic blood pressure deception test. It is a 'black box' which records changes in blood pressure, breathing rate and sweating, all of which may indicate that the suspect is stressed by some particular questions. This approach is based on the notion that a guilty party is more likely to manifest signs of stress than an innocent person. The possible use of the polygraph by intelligence agencies creates a moral dilemma, though, as it does not necessarily produce consistently reliable results. British agencies tend to be dismissive of the value of polygraphs. Sir Maurice Oldfield, Chief of SIS, swore to me that he had outwitted one. However, while they certainly cannot be considered to be lie detectors, they may provide useful indicators of subjects deserving further examination.

The 'black box' style of polygraph appeared in the first half of the twentieth century, publicly championed by Professor Leonard Keeler of Northwestern University in the US. Keeler's view in 1930 was that the only torture involved in such tests were self-induced through fear of being caught, a fear which, in any case, was likely to be present in the mind of any guilty party whatever the form of interrogation. Another

US academic, William Marston, agreed with Keeler's views but went further in claims for the polygraph. He argued that the polygraph test should be administered to every candidate for public office.[10]

While the British have been averse to the polygraph, the Americans have used and studied it widely. The Israeli and Japanese police routinely use the polygraph for investigations and have reported considerable success both in identifying criminals and exonerating the innocent. In an article in the *Journal of Applied Psychology* by Vance MacLaren of the University of New Brunswick, it is argued that if what the author calls the Guilty Knowledge Test is used skilfully it can produce useful results, reporting that in one experiment 76 per cent of those with 'secret knowledge' were correctly identified. Nonetheless, the results overall, whether from laboratory tests or practice, do not support the view that the polygraph will necessarily detect a lie.

Oversight, Freedom of Information and Security

'I think there's a tradition that the CIA is a silent service, and it's a good one. I think the silence ought to begin with me.'

Richard Helms, when appointed DCI in 1966

'I recall only two instances in intelligence history in which the files of intelligence services were as thoroughly ransacked as those of the Agency during [the mid-1970s congressional] investigations.'

Richard Helms, former DCI, 2003

'95 percent of what leaks comes out of the executive branch, because some people believe they have some free right to disseminate this information.'

George Tenet, DCI, 1999

The requirements of security do not sit easily with demands for transparency and political oversight of intelligence agencies and their work in a democracy. To give parliamentarians access to classified material so that they may monitor the intelligence agencies' actions necessarily entails a risk to the security of that material. Yet the UK maintains a parliamentary oversight committee, and the US has a comparable system.

No doubt a lot of time is spent on oversight and freedom of information issues, which might, perhaps, be better spent, but the British parliamentarians charged with scrutiny have shown more restraint and concern for national security than their colleagues in the US. We have never had the equivalent of the Church Committee rampaging like a rogue elephant in the delicate world of espionage. It is ironic that the CIA, which in the 1960s, as a result of the Philby case, was chary of sharing secrets with their leaky cousins in the UK, became a major security risk because of the antics of egocentric US politicians just a few years later.

George Bush Snr, former President as well as former DCI, said on 26 April 1999 at the dedication ceremony for the George Bush Centre for Intelligence at the CIA, 'I have nothing but contempt and anger for those who betray our trust by exposing the names of our sources. They are, in my view, the most insidious of traitors.' The list of criticisms by former DCIs could, of course, be much longer. Bill Colby, who was at the helm when the oversight frenzy was gathering momentum, had to spend far more of his time attending meetings with members of Congress and Senators than on directing the CIA. The unfortunate Colby was a superb and experienced intelligence operator, as well as an admirable human being. He was excoriated by many of his colleagues for giving too much information to the politicians. His response, which seemed to make sense, was that had he not cooperated there would have been a flood of subpoenas and contempt citations, and the damage to the Agency would have been far greater. Alas, the damage can never be entirely undone; allies and agents have learnt that the well established 'need to know' principle is no longer sacrosanct in a democratic society where freedom can easily turn into licence and transparency takes precedence over security.

Traditionally, Britain has been secretive about intelligence. Until late in the twentieth century the very existence of MI5, SIS and GCHQ was unacknowledged. Questions put to the government were answered with the bland, 'we do not comment on intelligence matters.' By the end of the century their existence had been acknowledged and their charters formalised and published. The Freedom of Information Act passed in 2000 includes references to intelligence, Special Forces, and provides for exemptions. The British, when making provision for exemptions, take into consideration a wide range of factors including possible damage to relations with other countries and their intelligence services. Long may common-sense prevail.

The Intelligence and Security Committee of Parliament (ISC), the UK's formal intelligence oversight body, was reformed by the Justice and

Security Act 2013 so that it has greater powers to collect evidence from the intelligence agencies. Even before this reform the ISC received visitors from other states wanting to learn from our model for the oversight of intelligence in a democratic state. While increased openness facilitates oversight by the ISC, the public and the media, there are others who argue that this damages the nation's security. There is no obvious way to resolve this tension between secrecy and accountability in intelligence.

A notable instance of this conflict arose when I was secretary at a meeting of the heads of the intelligence services at which the main subject on the agenda was the growing pressure to release information on the successes of British intelligence in the Second World War. Silence had been maintained for twenty-five years, and no official was anxious to change the rules. Silence seemed preferable to the unknown consequences of change. Outside Whitehall, however, change was already taking place. David Kahn's book *The Codebreakers* and Donald MacLachlan's book *Room 39* had already been published.[11] Others were waiting in the wings anxious to publish on the basis of their wartime experiences, most notably Sir John Masterman, formerly Provost of Worcester College, Oxford. Masterman, wartime intelligence officer, Christ Church historian, cricketer and novelist, wanted to tell the world about the remarkable triumphs of British intelligence in the Second World War. He proposed to do so in a book entitled *The Double-Cross System*, which he based (rather cheekily) on the official report he had written at the end of the war about the operations that had comprehensively bamboozled German intelligence over our military plans and strength (see Chapter Twelve).[12]

The committee complained that Masterman was letting the side down and should not be allowed to publish. In 1972, after much huffing and puffing and even threats of prosecution, he was given permission. The unkind suggested that he was helped by the fact that both Sir Alec Douglas-Home, a future Prime Minister, and Sir Dick White had been his pupils at Oxford. Alternatively, it can be argued that commonsense prevailed.

However, the Masterman item was only the hors d'oeuvre at this meeting. The main issue on the agenda was the argument about whether intelligence should be given its place among all the other official volumes being published about the history of the Second World War. The committee were adamant that no official history should be written on so delicate a subject, and in any case would be impossible to write.

Taking a deep breath, I ventured to say that I thought that posterity would not be very kind to us if the minutes showed that the proposal had been vetoed before any research had been done. Should we not call upon an eminent historian to look at the records, and if they recommended that something could be done, they could be commissioned to write a secret history, which would not have to be published? To my delight the committee agreed that Professor Harry Hinsley should be invited to look into the matter. The result was the publication of three volumes on intelligence and one on strategic deception. They are heavy going; cattily described as history written in committee for committees. Nevertheless, they have ensured that the role of intelligence in World War II has been recorded.[13] A small collection of other official or authorised histories of intelligence have followed, including Christopher Andrew's *The Defence of the Realm*.[14] Common sense has prevailed over a bureaucratic lethargy that was hiding under the cloak of security.

Blackmail, Drugs and Sex

'[T]he Female of Her Species is more deadly than the Male.'

Rudyard Kipling, 'The Female of the Species', 1911

British intelligence has never officially accepted such infelicitous improprieties as intelligence brothels, blackmail, and the use of drugs as appropriate weapons for their armoury. These weapons, along with assassination, continue however to be frequently used by others.[15] Such subjects have been taught in the Andropov School for Intelligence Officers in Moscow, where the tradition that predates the Russian Revolution of using any weapon, from torture through to sex and blackmail, has been continued. They do not appear in the syllabus at British intelligence schools, and they certainly are not 'cricket'.

The drugging of a courier or a potential agent with a view to subsequent blackmail is unlikely to lead to the blossoming of a warm and trusting relationship between case officer and agent. The frightened agent, recruited through fear of exposure, is unlikely to be whole-heartedly devoted to serving the interests of his or her blackmailers. The perception of a change in the terrorist threat brought about by 9/11 has renewed debates about whether these methods are acceptable.

Sex is a questionable basis for an intelligence relationship. Seduction has never been a formally recognised weapon in the British intelligence armoury. After the Second World War, however, attractive, vivacious, young ballerinas were to be found at official receptions in Moscow and Leningrad, enchanting the unattached male guests. They often ensnared besotted diplomats. Not every 'swallow', to use the Russian jargon, succeeded, but many did. For example, in 1953 the CIA's first Station Chief—their most senior representative—in Moscow was sent home in disgrace, having succumbed to the charms of a swallow; eleven members of the US Embassy staff were also sent home during the same period for the same reason. During this period the French Ambassador and his Air Attaché also succumbed to the charms of swallows.

This was a time when, in Western society, homosexuality was still regarded in much the same terms as it had been when Oscar Wilde was condemned. So the 'sex' weapon was doubly powerful in the case of a homosexual entrapment. Before the First World War, Colonel Redl of the Austrian General Staff, an extravagant dandy and a homosexual had been trapped by the Russian Imperial Intelligence Services with money and with the threat of exposing his sexual orientation. Redl gave the Russians total access to the secrets of the Austrian General Staff and his material was rated as being worth at least twelve divisions.

Crude Soviet provocation tactics often worked: a frequent ploy was to lure a foolish foreigner into bed with a swallow and then send in an angry 'husband', complete with camera, ready to photograph the seducer *in flagrante delicto*. He would be threatened with exposure to his Ambassador if he refused to collaborate. The approach would not, of course, have worked had the victims felt confident that if they made an honest confession to their Ambassador the only result would be a reprimand. However, Western intelligence services were so anxious about blackmail that a confession would almost certainly lead to immediate repatriation and a serious black mark.

During the Cold War period the acknowledged masters of sex ploys were the East German Service. Markus Wolf, the East German Chief's, first essay into the use of sex to produce intelligence was, however, a farce. His Soviet advisers had helped him to set up a *malina* (slang for a 'honey trap'), a brothel equipped with concealed microphones and cameras in order to entrap foreign staff. Finding swallows proved to be difficult. Wolf's first team were so unattractive that they had to be dismissed; a second team was infested with lice. Then the *malina* and its staff waited in vain for a visitor. Eventually one of Wolf's staff managed to persuade a West German journalist to enter the trap, but the journalist spent the evening sitting in the kitchen chatting to a maid. Yet Wolf was lucky; the journalist guessed the true nature of the *malina*, offered his services and became quite useful.

The East German Service went on to penetrate the Bonn Government at many levels. The basic ploy was simple; their officers were sent to cafés near ministries and government offices, which were regularly used by their employees, to pick up junior female staff. If a suitable lonely heart was found, the next stage was to deepen the relationship and to seek help from the new found friend under some innocent sounding pretext, gradually leading to a compromising situation and, finally, to recruitment. The East German officers were not specially selected Adonis types, trained in *ars amatoria*. But they were good listeners and, perhaps, amateur psychologists, using friendship, sometimes even marriage, as a weapon. The German service was even prepared to organise a bogus religious marriage if need be. As KGB's Major General Oleg Kalugin remarked, sex could indeed be a powerful weapon.

Conclusion

There is a balance to be struck between ethics and the requirements of intelligence. Of intelligence's moral dilemmas it is perhaps interrogation and torture that are given the most attention today. There are, unsurprisingly, polarised opinions on what is effective, what is permissible, and what is required in terms of interrogation practices. More research needs to be done on what methods are effective and acceptable.

This chapter has discussed just some of the moral dilemmas of intelligence. The issue of the enormous thefts of classified material, as carried out by Edward Snowden and Chelsea (formerly Bradley) Manning must also be debated more seriously. The public must be left in no doubt as to the damage to our national security done by all such whistleblowers.

PART THREE

FAMOUS CASES OF INTELLIGENCE IN PRACTICE

8

PEARL HARBOR

.

'The Japanese are not going to risk a fight with a first-class nation.'

Charles S. Faddis, US Congressman, February 1941

'No matter what happens the U.S. Navy is not going to be caught napping.'

Frank Knox, Secretary of the US Navy, 4 December 1941

The attack on the US naval base at Pearl Harbor on the Hawaiian island of Oahu was undoubtedly a victory for the Japanese. Broad intelligence warnings that the Japanese were preparing for war reached US customers yet they paid scant attention. It was an intelligence failure for the US in the broad sense that the intelligence community failed to persuade the politicians and military commanders to expect a Japanese attack. Their general warnings should not have been brushed aside so easily.

There are parallels between Pearl Harbor in December 1941 and the Al Qaeda attacks of 9/11. Each came as a horrific surprise. Japanese naval aircraft destroyed over 200 planes and ships, and killed around 2,500 service personnel at Pearl Harbor; the Al Qaeda attack, using four civilian airliners as flying bombs, killed over 3,000 civilians.

In both cases alarm bells had been sounding, but had not rung insistently enough to engender a sense of urgency or a drastic review of the defensive measures in place. There was no top priority requirement demanding special efforts by all agencies to identify the nature of the threat. It was not until after the disasters that a sense of urgency was shared by all agencies concerned, and that analysts identified potentially useful minute pieces of intelligence as wheat among the mass of chaff. The Pearl Harbor attack demonstrates the sins of assessment discussed in an earlier chapter. Above all, it shows how almost impossible it is to persuade senior officers to overcome their prejudices and preconceptions. This, and the cases in the remaining chapters in this part of the book, are well-known and much analysed.

The background to the attack was Japan's insistence that the West tolerate its expansionist policies, which were designed to give it access to oil, rubber and other strategic materials. The determination of the Japanese to break out of their economic straitjacket does not seem to have been adequately understood, although they had joined Germany's Axis grouping in September 1940. The West had no hard secret intelligence on their plans or intentions: a Sigint indication that Pearl Harbor might be the object of a surprise attack was not passed on to the American military commanders in Hawaii.

The failure to foresee and warn of the possibility of a full-scale air assault on Pearl Harbor ranks high in the annals of intelligence failures, but, as usual, the responsibility for the disaster lay at many doors. From President Franklin Roosevelt downwards the idea of such an air attack was unthinkable. Security in Japan had prevented foreigners from observing their preparations, and the weather helped conceal their armada during its journey to the target. Yet there was plenty of overt evidence of the belligerent state of mind of the Japanese. In January 1941, for example, the Japanese Foreign Minister bluntly announced that Japan 'must control the Western Pacific.'

Another factor contributing to the disaster was a lack of coordination and communication between departments in Washington and Pearl Harbor. The general chairing the Army Board of Inquiry that looked into this surprise attack remarked of the Pearl Harbor warning systems and information centre, 'it all seems cock-eyed to me.' Complacency and racial arrogance were also part of the problem.

Further, historical precedents seem to have been ignored. With British help, the Japanese had built up a formidable modern navy which fifty years before had blown the fleets of Imperial China and Imperial Russia out of the water, and the Japanese had a strong martial culture. Yet sheer astonishment seems to have been the order of the day when reports were first received of the devastating air attack on Oahu.

The Events of 1941: Prelude to War

In mid-1941 Admiral Isoroku Yamamoto, Commander of the Japanese Combined Fleet, proposed that Pearl Harbor should be attacked and the core of the US Pacific Fleet destroyed. His colleagues considered that an attack on Hawaii would be foolhardy and Yamamoto only got his way by threatening to resign. The Japanese operation was a gamble since the voyage from Japan to the launching position, 200 miles north of Hawaii, would take ten days. The task force, covering an area of 5 square miles, might be spotted by air reconnaissance and the weather might have been so rough that the ships could not refuel en route.

The Japanese Naval Task Force sent to Pearl Harbor consisted of two battleships, six aircraft carriers, three cruisers, eleven destroyers, eight supply vessels, and a fleet of submarines, five of which had midget submarines strapped like papooses on their backs. The air armada consisted of 355 warplanes; bombers, dive-bombers, torpedo bombers and forty-five Zero-type fighters whose pilots had honed their skills in battle over China.

General Walter Short, commander of the US Army's Hawaiian Department, assumed that the only threat facing the naval base at Pearl Harbor was sabotage or surreptitious entry by submarine. An assault by air was considered impossible because of distance. Admiral Husband Kimmel, CINCPAC, was thinking about sea battles, not the defence of Pearl Harbor. The FBI's representative in Hawaii had proposed curbing the flagrant intelligence collection activities being brazenly carried out by the Japanese Consulate's intelligence officers. But Short insisted that the consulate must not be restricted in its activities for fear of losing the support of the local Japanese community. It should have been obvious that the Japanese were being forced into a corner, and one did not have to be a Japanese expert to work out that Japan would not surrender without a fight.

The Attack

At 5.30 a.m. on Sunday 7 December 1941 two Japanese aircraft were launched to discover whether the Pacific Fleet was still in Harbor. They returned undetected, and reported that the battleships were in Harbor and the carriers at sea. The first air fleet then took off, followed by the second air fleet half an hour later.

There had been a few alarms and excursions during the night before the attack, which should have alerted the US garrison. Destroyers had sighted and sunk midget submarines, and the radar operator had reported a mass of aircraft approaching. But these incidents were not correctly interpreted.

The base was totally surprised by the attack. Kimmel had given little thought to defence of the base. He had a formidable fleet. It included three carriers, twenty-nine destroyers, eight battleships and numerous cruisers and submarines. Yet despite receiving a 'war' warning from Washington no action was taken to step up air patrols.

So the battleships remained in Harbor, aircraft were huddled together to facilitate defence against saboteurs, ammunition was not positioned ready for action, and servicemen were on weekend leave. The Japanese were presented with sitting ducks in the Harbor and on the airfields. By the end of the attack 188 warplanes and eighteen warships, including eight battleships were out of action, and almost 2,500 US personnel had been killed. The following chronology of the lead up to the attack and of the attack itself presents some of the key pieces of information that might have been interpreted as indications that Japan was preparing to attack the US and, more specifically, to attack Pearl Harbor. The US was not party to all of these pieces of information, but where it is known that they were in possession of these, it is noted below.

1941

January 27	US Ambassador in Tokyo, Joseph Grew, reports that his Peruvian colleague has heard of a Japanese intention to attack Pearl Harbor. This Rumint was dismissed by Naval Intelligence, whose view was that 'no move against Pearl Harbor [sic] appears imminent or planned for in the foreseeable future.'
July	The US freezes Japanese assets and, as revealed by Sigint, Ambassador Nomura, posted to London, is pessimistic about his mission.
September 4	The Japanese Cabinet approves a policy paper outlining the Japanese attitude towards the US and its European allies. It stated, '[i]n the event that there is no prospect of our demands being met by the first ten days of October … we will immediately decide

to commence hostilities'. The policy paper described 'Minimum Demands' and 'Maximum Concessions', and did not address Western demands for Japan to cease its belligerent policies in China and South East Asia.

September 12   War games in Tokyo cover all aspects of an attack on South East Asia including Pearl Harbor.

October 6   The Japanese Army High Command decides that war is inevitable.

October 16   A new Cabinet is in place in Tokyo. The US Government notes that it will be more anti-US than its predecessor.

October 17   US Army Intelligence lists the five most likely Japanese moves. An attack on the US is ranked last.

November 4   US intelligence notes that Japan is withdrawing all merchant shipping from the Western hemisphere.

November 5   A telephone tap intercepts a message from Tokyo to Nomura that said the deadline for settling the dispute with the US had been postponed from 25 to 29 November, but '[a]fter that things are going to happen automatically.'

November 14   US intelligence, confused by a torrent of repetitive Japanese signals, reports that the aircraft carriers 'remain relatively inactive', unaware that every operational carrier in the Japanese Navy had joined the Hawaiian Task Force in Hitokappu Bay.

November 15   A message from Tokyo to Nomura reconfirms that there would be no further negotiations after 25 November.

November 16   Captain Ellis Zacharias, US Navy, a Japanese specialist and former intelligence officer but now a Captain of a warship, tells colleagues that he expects the Japanese to start the war with a sneak attack, which would include an attack on Pearl Harbor. Zacharias had come to the correct conclusion by using open source information. Since he was outside the intelligence circle his conclusions carried no weight.

November 26/29   Sigint reports two directives (usually known as the 'Winds' messages) from Tokyo, which laid down that in an emergency Japanese news broadcasts would contain messages disguised as weather reports, to indicate the country with whom a diplomatic breach had occurred.

US Secretary of State Cordell Hull informs the Japanese that the US insists they withdraw from China, Indo China, and from their alliance with Germany and Italy.

The Japanese Task Force Commander, about to set sail for Oahu, seeks reassurance from Japanese intelligence that the US Fleet will be in Pearl Harbor on Sunday, 7 December. Agent Suzuki assures him that the fleet returns to base every weekend.

November 27   General George Marshall, the US Army's Chief of Staff, issues a 'war warning' message about Japanese future action being 'unpredictable but [noting that] hostile action [was] possible at any moment', and orders that reconnaissance be carried out.

November 28   US Sigint identifies further instructions from Tokyo to Honolulu to report in detail on movements of capital ships in and out of Pearl Harbor.

November 29   The US Army's periodic *Estimate of Threats* contains no mention of the possibility of an attack on Pearl Harbor. During the subsequent investigations G-2 explained this by reference to the conviction of their naval colleagues that because of the US Navy's disposition a Japanese attack would be either impractical or suicidal.

December 1   US intelligence notes a tightening of Japanese signal security, that the Japanese Navy are changing call signs with increasing frequency, and that it seems as if many ships are now maintaining total radio silence. Intelligence correctly interprets this as an ominous sign of imminent aggression, but Kimmel rejects proposals for special reconnaissance flights to search for the invisible fleet. He characterises his intelligence officer's interpretation as a case of crying wolf.

Sigint reports that Tokyo has ordered Japanese offices in London, Singapore, Hong Kong and Manila to destroy their cipher machines.

December 2   Lieutenant Commander Edwin Layton, Fleet Intelligence Officer, confirms to Kimmel that intelligence does not know the locations of the Japanese aircraft carriers.

December 3   The telephone tap on the Japanese Consulate in Hawaii records the voice of the cook informing a friend that the whole consulate staff was feverishly destroying documents and codebooks.

Washington informs Kimmel that the Japanese have been ordered to destroy all their confidential material, including codes and ciphers, at once. Kimmel did not pass the message on to General Short.

December 5   Sigint distributes a version of a message dated 29 November asking Honolulu to report details of ships in Pearl Harbor. This adds to the picture of an unhealthy Japanese intelligence interest in the ships deployed in the Harbor.

December 6   The chief of the US Sigint section was persuaded to approve an order to all stations in the Pacific and South East Asia to destroy surplus communications material.

December 7   *2 a.m.* Japanese intelligence reports that neither barrage balloons nor anti-torpedo nets were being used in Pearl Harbor.

3.57 a.m. US Minesweeper Condor reports a sighting of a periscope near the mouth of the Harbor.

6.30 a.m. A US supply ship reports to US Destroyer Ward a sighting of what seemed to be the conning tower of an unidentified submarine near the harbour.

6.40 a.m. A US Destroyer on patrol reports sinking a midget submarine just outside the harbour. This report was logged at 6.53 a.m., and was swiftly followed by a report from the air force that they had sunk a submarine one mile out from the harbour. In hindsight, these reports were a clear indication that there was mischief afoot, and could have given the garrison and the fleet lead-time to order action stations. But senior officers wanted verification, and the discovery of the midget submarine's attack did not trigger a general alert.

7.20 a.m. The radar operator reports that his screen shows an armada of aeroplanes 74 miles away. It was thought that they were US planes coming home.

7.30 a.m. (1 p.m. Washington time). The last of a fourteen-part message from the Japanese Government is conveyed to the US Government. It is a declaration that negotiations had been broken off, and recognised by the US leaders as tantamount to a declaration of war.

7.40 a.m. The Japanese Air Commander leading the armada fires his Verey pistol to start the attack.

7.50 a.m. The first bombs drop.

The Nature of the Intelligence Failure

With hindsight it is easy to identify moments when an imaginative and confident intelligence officer might have been prepared, despite the lack of hard intelligence on the Japanese war plans, to risk crying wolf and to insist that, not only was there a probability of Japan starting a war, but also that the plan might include an air assault on Pearl Harbor. While not all of the pieces of information given in the chronology above were known to the US at the time, many of them were.

A Senior National Intelligence Chief sitting alongside the President might have been able to persuade the US establishment to revise their view of the Japanese threat. Many of the causes of the intelligence failure at Pearl Harbor were the same as those which led to Malaya and Singapore being overrun in 1941, when the Japanese drove the much larger British Army down the Peninsula to ignominious surrender in Singapore. The culprits include arrogance, cultural stereotyping, groupthink and wishful thinking.

The West seemed to have been unbelievably arrogant and complacent in its assessment of the Japanese. The Japanese were despised by many as figures of fun; bandy legged, short sighted little men, in crumpled uniforms, who were not likely to give trouble to the armed forces of the West. So the news of the devastating attack on Pearl Harbor was received with incredulity. Frank Knox, Secretary of the Navy said, '[i]t can't be true.' General Douglas MacArthur chose to believe they must have been using white mercenary pilots. Presidential adviser Harry Hopkins remarked, 'there must be some mistake.' Just before the attack, President Roosevelt had expressed the opinion that Japan's military masters would not risk war with the US. The Japanese had been written off as mere imitators. In fact they had produced the best torpedo of that time, learning from the British success against the Italian Fleet in the shallow waters of Taranto. Their Zero fighter out-performed Western planes.

It is much more comfortable to accept the received wisdom of the society in which one operates, than to question it. Layton, Fleet Intelligence Officer, and an expert on the Japanese language, history and culture, was unable to make any impact on the groupthink of his colleagues in Pearl Harbor. To the group, it was so unlikely that the Japanese Navy would launch a surprise attack, that any indications they were wrong were unpalatable. It required the explosion of the Japanese bombs to open the US Navy's minds to the fact that the Japanese sailors and airmen were highly trained, skilled, and dangerous opponents.

It is natural that the diplomats should be asked to engage in negotiation to try to find a peaceful solution. This was the case with the US Government in 1941. Diplomats must, of course, remain optimistic in order to negotiate but they must also be careful that optimism does not mutate into over-sanguine interpretations of the attitude of the opposition.

This was an asymmetrical intelligence war. The Japanese had been given free rein in Hawaii to roam, fly aeroplanes and sail around taking photographs as they pleased. Their tactical intelligence was voluminous and accurate. Short was instructed by Washington to be careful not to antagonise the Japanese residents by imposing restrictions on movement.

In Japan, however, foreigners were forbidden to travel outside Tokyo, so they could not observe the training of low flying bombers or the assembly of a naval task force in the Kuril Islands north east of Japan. The FBI rejected Britain's offer of a source who had intelligence suggesting preparations were being made for an attack on Pearl Harbor. Dusko Popov, codenamed TRICYCLE, was a valuable British double agent, and had been asked by the Abwehr to report in detail on the ships in Pearl Harbor, and to find out all he could about the techniques which had enabled the British to sink the Italian Fleet at Taranto. Fortunately for the Japanese, Hoover, the FBI's Director, took an instant dislike to Popov and forbade the FBI from having any dealings with him.

There were Sigint successes that provided a timely account of the diplomatic messages passing between Tokyo and its Ambassadors and consulates, and this traffic included Japanese intelligence briefs for the intelligence officers in the Honolulu Consulate. These briefs showed that Tokyo had a huge appetite for detail on the type and location of ships in the Harbor, detail useful to someone compiling a picture of a potential target. The discovery of the Japanese briefs caused hardly a ripple when they might have been taken as an indicator of possible preparations for an attack. It was also unfortunate for the US that the replies to the intelligence briefs did not go back to Tokyo on the diplomatic circuit but on the more secure Japanese naval circuit. The result was that US intelligence only knew the questions being asked by Japanese intelligence but not the answers.

Japanese intelligence

The Japanese were as prone to foolish generalisations, stereotyping and hubris as the Anglo-Saxons. Admiral Yamamoto, although he had spent many years in the US as a student and at the Japanese Embassy, understood so little about the US temperament and psychology that he predicted that a successful Japanese assault on Pearl Harbor would persuade the US that the Japanese were too strong to fight.

Since the Japanese had confined foreigners to Tokyo, it was easy to conceal the intensive activity that preceded the attack on Pearl Harbor. Japanese citizens and their controlled press did not need to be reminded to keep quiet. As it was, the Japanese did not need a complex deception plan, only a confusion plan. Aircraft carriers and warships were shuffled about, and task forces only assembled at the eleventh hour. Normal leave patterns continued until the last moment, suggesting business as usual in the fleet. Task forces were issued with cold weather as well as hot weather uniforms.

Nonetheless, the fleet's observance of radio silence was a major element in the Japanese security plan. In the weeks before the surprise attack call signs were changed with increasing frequency and radio messages endlessly repeated, thus overloading the decrypting and linguistic resources of the small US Sigint sections, and frustrating attempts to maintain up-to-date accurate plots of naval deployments. Finally, the exhausted Siginters were frustrated by total radio silence within the Hawaiian Task Force at sea, which communicated only by flags during the day, and by shaded signal lights at night.

Conclusion

This well-known case of intelligence failure demonstrates many of the challenges of intelligence work. There was an institutional failure within American military intelligence to accept that there was a serious military threat. Like their British colleagues in Singapore, they believed that they were an impregnable fortress and that the Japanese were not a serious adversary. The central cause of the debacle was unwillingness on the part of most of the intelligence and operational staffs to open their minds to new facts and ideas. Pearl Harbor, they thought, could not conceivably be on the Japanese list of immediate targets.

It would have been difficult for US intelligence to discover the Japanese target and the date of the attack, and this should be borne in mind when assessing the overall failure of the US to accept that a Japanese attack might take place. Sigint did well by providing evidence of Japanese intelligence interest in Pearl Harbor, but even if Sigint coverage had been significantly better, it would have had little effect on the situation since Japanese radio silence would have defeated the Sigint staff. Of course the sort of dominance that the Allies achieved over the Germans would only have been possible had the Japanese given the Allies a present by discussing their most secret plans by radio.

So the blame for the lack of urgency must be shared throughout the whole intelligence community. Kimmel and Short were, rightly in my opinion, blamed for failing to consider whether in the light of the 'war warnings', however general, they should put the base on a war footing. Strategic warnings of a possible attack by the Japanese ought to have been acted on and the ships and aircraft at Pearl Harbor made less vulnerable. There was one other important familiar culprit though: the common tendency of operational staff to look down on the backroom intelligence staff. This serves as a reminder that for intelligence to achieve its potential, it is not only the intelligence staff who need to be good at their jobs but the consumers of intelligence too.

9

CUBA

THE BAY OF PIGS AND THE MISSILE CRISIS

'[V]ictory has 100 fathers and defeat is an orphan.'

President Kennedy, 1961

'How could I have been so stupid, to let them go ahead?'

President Kennedy after the Bay of Pigs disaster

'Plausible denial was a pathetic illusion.'

Lyman Kirkpatrick, CIA Inspector General, October 1961

'About 3,500 agent and refugee reports were analyzed ... and of this number, only eight in retrospect were considered as reasonably valid indicators of the development of offensive missiles in Cuba.'

John McCone, DCI, 1962

What the Bay of Pigs case of 1961 illustrates above all is the difficulty of attempting to bring about regime change. It was a half-hearted effort to do so using an under-resourced invasion force very thinly disguised as indigenous counter-revolutionaries, and was an unmitigated disaster.

The Cuban Missile Crisis of the following year was of a very different nature: since it ended without major engagement, it teaches different lessons. It brought the world to the brink of a nuclear war, and demonstrated the difficulty of discovering the intentions of the enemy. The Soviets and the Americans were dangerously ignorant of each other's mindsets.

Both cases illustrate the particular difficulty of validating human intelligence when the sources are exiles. They also recognise that Rumint and Hunchint have useful roles to play. The two Cuban cases were also significantly linked in terms of outcome: the Bay of Pigs disaster of 1961 led to a lack of confidence in the intelligence provided by Cuban sources, and to excessive confidence in the part of Cuba and their Soviet allies, a confidence which went on to affect the course of the Cuban Missile Crisis.

The Bay of Pigs Disaster

Fidel Castro ousted Cuban dictator General Batista in 1959 and President Eisenhower came to view Castro's new government with increasing unease. On 17 March 1960 Eisenhower ordered the CIA to produce a plan to overthrow the Cuban leader. Richard Bissell, the CIA's Deputy Director of Plans, proposed to recruit, arm and train an expeditionary 'Brigade' of around 1,500 Cuban exiles, equip them with landing craft, guns and tanks, transport them to Cuba by a flotilla of merchant ships, and support them with sixteen ex-US Air Force B-26 bombers. Operation Pluto would begin two days before the invasion, when the B-26 bombers would be launched from Nicaragua in order to destroy Castro's air force. The invasion flotilla would leave Nicaragua the following day. Early on the day of the invasion the Brigade would land undetected by Castro's armed forces. Bissell envisaged that should the CIA-led invasion fail to bring about the immediate downfall of Castro, the Brigade would establish a guerrilla base in the hills and fight on.

The plan was drastically and probably fatally amended when President Kennedy decided that the chosen landing point was unsuitable. Bissell offered the Bay of Pigs, around sixty miles to the west of the town of Trinidad, as an alternative. The Bay of Pigs, as the US was to learn the hard way, was operationally unsuitable. It had not been reconnoitred and was full of submerged rocks. In addition, the Zapata Swamp behind the Bay of Pigs was not a suitable base for guerrilla operations and favoured the defending forces.

On 15 April 1961 at 2 a.m., the pilots of the Brigade air force at Puerto Cabeza, Nicaragua, set off to attack the Cuban air force not knowing that Castro, anticipating air attack, had dispersed his planes.

Two B-26 bombers, two Sea Furies and two T-33 jets survived the attack. The Cubans and their international sympathisers ridiculed the cover story that anti-Castro defectors from the Cuban air force had flown the B-26s involved in the attack. Kennedy then decided to prohibit any further B-26 operations thus giving the freedom of the skies to Castro's planes.

During the early hours of Monday 17 April, the invasion force began to land despite encountering jagged masses of coral. At dawn the Cuban air force arrived to strafe the beachhead and two ships from the invading forces' flotilla were sunk and the rest were driven away. Although the invading Brigade fought hard it became increasingly evident that their 1,500 men would, before long, be overwhelmed by the weight of the counterattack. The Brigade fought on, but by the end of three days the Cubans had captured most of them and Operation Pluto was over.

The performance of intelligence and its customers

It is difficult to know where to start a critique of this disaster as there were a number of intelligence failings. One of these was that the plan assumed Castro's intelligence was so ineffective that the invasion would benefit from total surprise. This was incorrect. Had the US known more about Cuban intelligence, they might not have misjudged their chances of achieving surprise. They also misjudged international opinion and assumed that the world would believe they had no part in the operation. Instead, there was a howl of global protest after the rebels bombed Cuba, and the US was embarrassed by its involvement in the failed invasion.

Much of the Humint on the strength of anti-Castro sentiment in Cuba was suspect because Exint had been given undue weight. Bissell failed to acknowledge that the informants had nothing to lose if the invasion failed and ignored the strong possibility that this intelligence was wildly optimistic. Bissell was also responsible for a failure of coordination within the CIA: he had excluded the CIA's Intelligence Directorate from the planning process thus denying his team independent validation and assessment.

There were also failures of coordination between the CIA and others. Perhaps the most crippling flaw in the plan was the unspoken assumption that, if the invasion stalled, Kennedy would allow US regular forces to join the battle. He did not, and this matter ought to have been clarified by the CIA before the invasion went ahead.

We can also criticise the decision to launch this military operation without directly involving the US military. The Special Operations chapter engages at greater length with the issue of who should be involved and responsible for such activities. The Cuban 'Brigade' who fought for the US in the invasion were, however, well trained. Their US advisers succeeded in this respect.

A far-reaching implication of the Bay of Pigs fiasco was that it led Soviet premier Nikita Khrushchev to believe that Kennedy, the young new President of the US, was a weakling and would not react forcibly to Soviet military provocation in Cuba. The invasion confirmed Castro's view that the US would stop at nothing in their attempts to destroy him, and he therefore welcomed a Soviet military presence. This presence took the form of Soviet missiles in Cuba.

The Cuban Missile Crisis

'We're eyeball to eyeball, and I think the other fellow just blinked.'

> Dean Rusk, Secretary of State, when Soviet ships turned round before reaching the US's blockade around Cuba, 1962

'Nuclear catastrophe was hanging by a thread … and we weren't counting days or hours, but minutes.'

> Anatoly Gribkov, Soviet general, 1962

When the Cuban Missile Crisis took place in October 1962 for a moment it looked as if the world might become embroiled in a Third World War; this time fought not with conventional armaments but with atomic weapons. This tense confrontation between the US and the Soviet Union is well documented. The US intelligence community had reported the growing Soviet presence in Cuba and the deployment of defensive SAMs there, but Humint reporting evidence of the deployment of MRBMs was not believed. Only one voice opposed this complacency: John McCone, Director of the CIA from November 1961 to April 1965, thought that the Soviets would exploit their opportunities in Cuba to the full and deploy MRBMs and ICBMs there. He did not make the mistake of mirror imaging that would have seen him assume that the Soviets would be thinking and behaving like the US in an analogous situation. Nor did he allow wishful thinking to influence his judgement.

On 15 October 1962, US aerial photographs showed that the Soviets were preparing sites designed to house ICBMs in Cuba, thus changing the nature of the threat to the US since such missiles, based in Cuba, would enable the Soviet Union to threaten the US homeland. The prospect of a nuclear Armageddon, which had dominated strategic planning since 1945, was no longer a theoretical scenario but an immediate danger.

Kennedy assembled a War Cabinet and, after days of tense discussion, issued an ultimatum to Premier Khrushchev, calling upon him to abandon his plans to deploy ICBMs to Cuba. The President announced that the US Navy would enforce a blockade to prevent further shipments of missile-related supplies. For two weeks there was a stand-off. Tension was increased when on 27 October Soviet SAMs shot down an American U-2 'spy plane' over Cuba. On 28 October Khrushchev and Kennedy reached an agreement and the crisis was ended.

The performance of intelligence

As early as 22 August 1962, the CIA had noted unprecedented activity in Cuba and reported that 'clearly something new and different is taking place.' In mid-September, however, a National Intelligence Estimate concluded that the deployment of nuclear missiles would be 'incompatible with Soviet practice to date and with Soviet policy as we presently estimate it.' In mid-October McGeorge Bundy, the President's security adviser, said on television, 'I think there is no present likelihood that the Cubans and the Cuban government and the Soviet government would in combination attempt to install a major offensive capability.' In short, American policymakers found it inconceivable that the Soviets would do anything as irresponsible as deploying intercontinental missiles in the US's backyard.

The US was reluctant to believe that the Soviets would behave in an egregiously aggressive fashion in Cuba. This was wishful thinking. Their intelligence community also seems to have been guilty of mirror imaging based on their belief that the US would not have indulged in so provocative an action close to the Soviet Union's borders. It is odd that despite decades of experience of the workings of the Soviet mind, American analysts were so easily persuaded that the Soviets thought as they did.

Intelligence, albeit belatedly, made a significant contribution when in mid-October air photography confirmed McCone's hunch that the

Soviets would install MRBMs and ICBMs in Cuba, but it came as a surprise to the US. The Soviets were installing weapons that would give them the ability to strike at any target in the US. But Imint had nothing to contribute to the debate about Khrushchev's thought processes, however, and his motives for installing the MRBMs and ICBMs were not known.

During the Missile Crisis that ensued, Robert Kennedy, US Attorney General, was in discreet contact with the Soviet Ambassador and assumed that he was telling him the truth. Even if that assumption had been correct, it did not guarantee that the Ambassador knew the whole story. On 26 October the Soviets opened a further 'back channel'. The KGB Resident in Washington, Counsellor Alexander Fomin, invited John Scali, a senior US journalist, to meet him urgently and suggested a solution which would include dismantling and removing the Soviet missiles if the US would promise not to invade Cuba. Scali passed this message to Rusk, who responded immediately with an oral message indicating that the US might be interested. Khrushchev then sent a conciliatory letter to Kennedy in which he acknowledged the Soviet missile build up in Cuba.

Any tendency to euphoria vanished when a second letter arrived from Khrushchev stating that in return for a Soviet withdrawal from Cuba they wanted the withdrawal of American missiles from Turkey. Kennedy ignored this letter, and offered a compromise along the lines suggested in the first Fomin meeting. On Sunday 28 October Khrushchev and Kennedy reached an agreement and the Crisis was resolved.

The US's misreading of the situation and incorrect assumptions can be summarised as follows: first, it was thought that the Soviets would only put defensive weapons in Cuba. Mirror imaging again. Second, it was assumed that the Kremlin would not delegate authority to use SAMs to local commanders in Cuba. Yet this is what happened. Third, the US thought that the firing of the SAMs, which shot down a U-2 over Cuba, was a deliberate gesture of escalation, when in fact it was the result of local initiative by a Soviet officer, not of a Kremlin ploy. Fourth, it was thought that Khrushchev's conciliatory letter of 28 October was a deception ploy. In truth it was a genuine climb down.

There were, however, some crucial intelligence successes for the West. Penkovsky, the GRU Colonel and the UK's star source, provided photographs of the various stages in the construction of a Soviet missile base. These enabled US analysts to ascertain which types of missiles the

Soviets were installing in Cuba and how close they were to being ready to fire. He also provided a salutary corrective to over-pessimistic western assessments of the Soviets' military capabilities. Their quality control was weak and their missiles of uncertain reliability.

The Soviets made many errors too. They assumed, for instance, that the MRBMs and ICBMs in Cuba would not be detected until they were ready for action. Castro and his fledgling intelligence service also misread the situation. They knew of a US contingency plan to attack Cuba, and were inclined to believe the US was willing to invade. In short, all three participants misunderstood the position of the other players. It was something of a miracle that, despite these major misunderstandings, the world escaped a nuclear war. There are, therefore, many useful lessons to be learnt from this much-analysed near catastrophe.

Conclusion

The dangers of mirror imaging and wishful thinking are all too evident in the US assessments that the Humint indicating the Soviet Union was installing MRBMs in Cuba was unreliable. It was Imint that finally convinced them there was a problem. Until then the general inclination among US intelligence and policymakers was to assume that the Soviets were only installing defensive systems.

Intelligence on intentions was lacking throughout. The US had little or no knowledge of whether the Soviet Union intended to use the MRBMs and ICBMs being constructed in Cuba to attack the US. But intelligence proved particularly valuable when, with Penkovsky's assistance, the US interpreted the aerial photographs, helping them to understand that the MRBMs were still under construction and not yet ready to launch. Intelligence, in Helms' words, 'bought [Kennedy] the time he needed.'

The Bay of Pigs disaster provides further examples of timeless errors. Presidents Eisenhower and Kennedy were naïve when they clung to their optimistic belief that the hand of the American government could be plausibly concealed in Operation Pluto. It is also difficult to forgive Kennedy's decision, as the invasion was about to start, to prohibit a second air attack. This points to a lack of effective communication and coordination between the President and the CIA. It also demonstrates the embarrassment that can be caused by an operation that is based on insufficient intelligence. A better understanding of the landing site at the Bay of Pigs, and knowledge that Cuba had anticipated an invasion, would have cast doubt on the wisdom of going ahead with it.

10

IRAQ

THE INTELLIGENCE IMBROGLIO
AND THE BUTLER REVIEW

'[W]e were nearly all wrong.'

David Kay, Head of Iraq Survey Group, 2004

'[Governments'] credible claims on our political loyalty have something to do with a demonstrable attention to truth, even unwelcome truth.'

Rowan Williams, Archbishop of Canterbury, 2004

'The JIC ... emerges as a craven creature that allowed the government's presentational priorities to take precedence over cautious and balanced assessment.'

Professor Eunan O'Halpin, 2005

'[T]he human intelligence that we had was modest and ... the nonhuman intelligence was dealing with a very hard target with a lot of underground capability... There were some things we knew quite a bit about and a lot of things we knew precious little about.'

Donald Rumsfeld, former Secretary of Defence

'Our intelligence estimates are provided for the use of policymakers. They can be used in whole or in part. They can be ignored, torn up or thrown away, but they may not be changed.'

William H. Webster, DCI, 1988

In March 2003 a US-led coalition invaded Iraq. The military victory which followed the offensive was a model of its kind. Building a new democratic government, free from the control of Saddam Hussein's Baath Party, was to prove much more difficult. The well intentioned attempt might have had some hope of success had it been the brainchild of a colonial power committed to a long stay, first as a government. There was really no hope that so drastic a change could be effected by bringing in advisers and pledging to leave as soon as possible. Anyone with some knowledge of such affairs could have predicted that the coalition was embarking on an impossible mission. It takes generations not years to change cultures, even if you have enough experts to bridge the cultural gaps.

The reputation of British intelligence was not enhanced by the Iraq affair. The British government built their case for war on intelligence assessments that claimed Iraq had a WMD capability. It appears that there was no such capability, that there had been tinkering with a JIC document, and that there had been a weakness in the validation process. It was alleged that intelligence had been 'sexed up' to suit the wish of the government, and so reviews were ordered. One was to be led by Lord Butler, a distinguished civil servant, who was tasked with reviewing intelligence on Iraqi WMD, and the other by Lord Hutton, a distinguished judge, who was asked to look into the circumstances surrounding the death of weapons expert Dr David Kelly. The Reviews drew back a small part of the veil which normally conceals the affairs of our secret agencies, and considerable heat was generated. The media predictably called the Reviews 'whitewashes'. Although they exonerated the intelligence community from the charge of bending intelligence to suit their political masters, they did contain several criticisms.

The rest of this chapter is concerned with the findings of the Butler Review, which commented on a range of important intelligence-related issues. I had the privilege of some discussion with Lord Butler at an Oxford Intelligence Conference. It was clear that, like Trend, he had a good feel for the intelligence business. It is a pity that neither was asked to conduct a serious study of the British intelligence system, and to push through needed reforms and improvements, which have yet to be carried out.

The Iraq imbroglio, the most recent of the cases in *Why Spy?*, took place at a time when I had been off the secret lists for over twenty years, although I continued to mix with intelligence professionals round the world, discussing assessments not secrets. As I write, Sir John Chilcot and the other members of the Iraq Inquiry are preparing their report. It is possible that they will comment on some of the aspects of the Iraq case included in this chapter. Rather than giving an overview of the whole affair,[1] the chapter focuses on some of the most valuable observations arising from this case and the Butler Review.

The Butler Review

The report published by Lord Butler drew on his committee's research and analysis of intelligence relating to Iraqi WMD. The quotes given below are taken from his report, and the numbers given relate to the paragraph numbers in the report's Summary of Conclusions. The fact that no heads rolled encouraged cries of 'cover up'. But few critics had taken the trouble to study the report in detail, and it was not a 'whitewash'. Extracts from the report are provided below so that readers can judge for themselves whether the 'whitewash' description was justified.

It would be impertinent to criticise the findings of the distinguished panel, particularly since they have had access to documents and witnesses not available to me. In any case, broadly speaking I agree with their findings; but I would like to see such reports written in plain English, so that the general public can get a clearer picture. In this case, as so often, the document is written in beautifully crafted mandarin prose that tends to obscure the reality and soften criticism.

Its conclusions on Humint included that:

14. After the departure of the United Nations [weapons] inspectors in December 1998, information sources were sparse...

15. The number of primary human intelligence sources remained few. ...

17. We do not believe that over-reliance on dissident and émigré sources was a major cause of subsequent weaknesses in the human intelligence relied on by the UK.

But there may have been over-reliance on reporting from Exint sources regarding the feelings of the Iraqi people. Exint was likely the source of the coalition's expectation that significant numbers of Iraqis would support them after the invasion. Exint, from whatever source—

émigrés, exiles or dissidents—contains an element of bias, vested interest, special pleading and so on, and must be treated with special care, as in the Bay of Pigs case. It is not difficult, however, to imagine the pressure on the intelligence community in the run up to the invasion, and the difficulty of finding reliable human sources in a rigidly controlled police state where the fate of those suspected of espionage was torture and death.

The Review also cast doubt on the validation process by which the reliability of Humint was judged. It stated:

16. Validation of human intelligence sources after the war has thrown doubt on a high proportion of those sources and of their reports…
    a. One SIS main source reported authoritatively on some issues, but on others was passing on what he had heard within his circle.
    b. Reporting from a sub-source to a second SIS main source … must be open to doubt.
    c. Reports from a third SIS main source have been withdrawn as unreliable.
    d. Reports from two further SIS main sources continue to be regarded as reliable, although it is notable that their reports were less worrying than the rest about Iraqi chemical and biological weapons capabilities.
    e. Reports received from a liaison service on Iraqi production of biological agent [sic] were seriously flawed…

Earlier validation had therefore been cast into doubt. The Review provided an explanation for this weakness:

19. …part of the reason for the serious doubt being cast over a high proportion of human intelligence reports on Iraq arises in weaknesses in the effective application by SIS of its validation procedures and in their proper resourcing. … We urge the Chief of SIS to ensure that this task is properly resourced and organised. …

The weak performance of the validation systems was related to the unfortunate fact that SIS had, for reasons of economy, abolished its requirements directorate and put requirements functions, which included validation of intelligence, into the operations arena. This meant that the SIS staff responsible for quality assurance had less power to question the validity of reports. Had a requirements directorate

existed and been doing its job, it would have been able to make a significant contribution to the validation process. To me and officers of my
generation this was a fundamental breach of the important convention
that operations people should not be the sole judges of their product.
The Butler Review noted this breach with tradition but made little of it.

It is evident that the intelligence material was weak. In effect there
was no hard evidence that Iraq had any WMD. The intelligence community did warn their customers of the uncertain nature of their intelligence, but predictably the customers were more interested in grabbing
intelligence straws which supported their views, than in underlining the
weakness of the evidence.

The fact that there were a number of secret reports suggesting that
Iraq had retained a WMD capability should have been set against the
fact that there was no hard evidence to support these reports. I had a
long session with a retired Israeli intelligence general who considered
that the JIC dossier on Iraqi WMD was an example of the tendency of
Western intelligence to be over-reliant on inductive reasoning. In this
case the fallacy ran 'Saddam Hussein's regime used to have WMD so
they probably still have.' My Israeli friend claimed that he had warned
Israeli intelligence that the claims in the JIC dossier should be taken
with a pinch of salt. The core problem was that the customers were
grasping for confirmation and had no interest in the inconvenient fact
that no reliable source had reported a sighting of WMD.

On technical expertise in the intelligence chain, the Butler Review
concluded:

59. We consider that further steps are needed to integrate the relevant
    work of the DIS [the Defence Intelligence Staff, the home of the
    government's scientific expertise] more closely with the rest of the
    intelligence community. ... If that involved increasing the Secret
    Intelligence Account ... we would support that.

I am not surprised that, having abolished the Cabinet Office's post of
Scientific Adviser, scientific and technical advice seem to have been miss-
ing in the final stages of the JIC's reporting. In my time we had Sir Alan
Cottrell as Scientific Adviser to help us. When the Cabinet Office was the
home of a Scientific Adviser, the JIC could consult them easily.

We still seem to lack a good system for pooling the talents on both
sides of the divide. Scientists can provide different perspectives. Their

input during the Iraq episode seems to have been small although the subject was technical. Had we still had a senior scientist in the Cabinet Office the story might have ended differently. The Review went on:

24. We accept the need for careful handling of human intelligence reports to sustain the security of sources. We have, however, seen evidence of difficulties that arose from the unduly strict 'compartmentalisation' of intelligence. ... arrangements should always be sought to ensure that the need for protection of sources should not prevent the exposure of reports on technical matters to the most expert available analysis.

The scientific experts were not fully used by the intelligence community.

The role of the JIC in the government's case for war in Iraq is perhaps the most controversial aspect of the Iraq case. The JIC authored a dossier entitled 'Iraq's Weapons of Mass Destruction', which was published by the government in September 2002. This act of publication was unprecedented. This dossier became, of course, the focus of media criticism. It was alleged that it had been 'sexed up' to make a stronger case, and that it was written to support the government's case for an invasion of Iraq. The Butler Review argued that neither of these allegations was true. But it was a serious departure from tradition to bring the JIC and its assessments into the public domain. Such adventures are best avoided: secret intelligence should remain secret, and the JIC's documents should remain secret too.

The JIC was, however, found to have performed well in many respects:

20. In general, we found that the original intelligence material was correctly reported in JIC assessments. An exception was the '45 minute' report. But this sort of example was rare.

21. ... we have found no evidence of deliberate distortion or culpable negligence.

22. We found no evidence of JIC assessments and the judgements inside them being pulled in any particular direction to meet the policy concerns of senior officials on the JIC.

The JIC was exonerated from any charges that they had adjusted their report or sexed it up to suit their customers. This was, in my opinion, charitable. It was not made abundantly clear to the customers how frail the evidence was. The '45 minute claim' became the subject of much media attention, and doubt was later cast on the dossier's claims that Iraq had chemical and biological weapons that could be deployed within 45 minutes. The dossier ought to have specified what type of weapons it referred to. There was not enough emphasis on the weakness of the evidence. The wording used was of considerable significance, producing an image of deadly immediate retaliation.

The Review's comments on the JIC performance include:

32. The JIC, with commendable motives, took responsibility for the dossier, in order that its content should properly reflect the judgements of the intelligence community. They did their utmost to ensure this standard was met. But this will have put a strain on them...

No doubt the JIC's motives were entirely honourable, but they should have rejected the idea of drafting a document for public consumption.

33. ...in translating material from JIC assessments into the dossier, warnings were lost about the limited intelligence base ... Language in the dossier may have left with readers the impression that there was fuller and firmer intelligence behind the judgements than was the case: our view ... is that judgements in the dossier went to (although not beyond) the outer limits of the intelligence available.

This is mandarin speak for 'the JIC were on the brink of exaggeration'.

The government's role in the September 2002 JIC dossier was also controversial. They were involved in the drafting of the dossier, and influenced the wording of the '45 minute claim'. The Butler and Hutton Reviews agree that the JIC only accepted the government's recommendations on the wording of the dossier when those suggestions were in keeping with the intelligence, and the grave charge against the JIC that they had succumbed to pressure from No. 10 Downing Street was not upheld.

The BBC asked at the time what my view was. I replied that I did not think that Trend would have allowed such interference in his day and I certainly thought it was wrong for No. 10 staff to have been involved in any way with the drafting of a JIC report. The situation was exacerbated by the exclusion of proper warnings about the reliability of intelligence on which the dossier's claims were based. It is difficult enough to educate lay customers in government so that they have a good understanding of the limitations of intelligence. It is impossible to educate the general public. But it was a bad precedent. No. 10 was a customer and had no business debating the draft with the producers. There will always be a suspicion of contamination, conscious or unconscious, when joint drafting takes place. It would be better if we stuck with DCI Webster's dictum that customers may reject, accept or ignore intelligence reports, but they must not alter them.

35. We conclude, with the benefit of hindsight, that making public that the JIC had authorship of the dossier was a mistaken judgement... the publication of such a document in the name and with the authority of the JIC had the result that more weight was placed on the intelligence than it could bear. The consequence also was to put the JIC and its Chairman into an area of public controversy and arrangements must be made for the future which avoid putting the JIC and its Chairman in a similar position.

37. ...if intelligence is to be used more widely by governments in public debate in future, those doing so must be careful to explain its uses and limitations. It will be essential, too, that clearer and more effective dividing lines between assessment and advocacy are established ...

The phrase 'more weight was placed on the intelligence than it could bear' is particularly obfuscatory. In plain English, the JIC report presented conclusions which would only have been valid had the intelligence reports been reliable. Since the intelligence was of doubtful validity, the conclusions were doubtful too. The JIC did not conceal the weakness of the intelligence base but neither did it emphasise it.

Conclusion

This was a classic case where reporting which seemed to confirm the received wisdom was welcomed almost unreservedly, whereas the absence of solid evidence was ignored. The Butler Review suggested that Humint on Iraqi WMD was of poor quality: the agents and sub-sources were reporting hearsay not information gathered by their own observation and direct knowledge. The intelligence professionals had warned the customers but failed to persuade them of the weakness of their intelligence. The JIC's customers should have been given more explicit warning about the weakness of the intelligence base on which the JIC had concluded that Iraq had WMD. There was no devil's advocate to attack the assessment, no bold spirit ready to incur the wrath of the government by suggesting that the Emperor had no clothes.

The shenanigans surrounding the drafting of the dossier should be avoided in future. This is a slippery slope leading to the infamous habits of dictators who, when faced with inconvenient intelligence, at best throw the intelligence away, at worst shoot the messenger. The job of intelligence is to discover the truth, however unpalatable, not to adjust the reporting to suit the customer.

The Butler Review did a good job. It might, however, have highlighted the failure to grapple with the subject of providing a structured career for specialist assessment officers. Progress has, however, been made, as a professional Head of Intelligence Analysis has since been appointed. It was almost forty years since Trend had pointed to the need to address this subject. The British intelligence system has been the envy of many countries who failed to find a way of bringing warring departments together into a central machine but there was, and still is, a lot to be done to improve the end product. The weakness caused in SIS's validation system by the false economy of abolishing the Directorate of Requirements was noted by the Review, but the serious implications of such a change were not. The savings derived from abolishing the independent Requirements Directorate in SIS have cost us a lot. When looking through the voluminous reporting after 9/11, I noted how often the official responsible referred to shortcomings that had been highlighted in previous reviews, which had not been dealt with. Let us hope that, as appears to be the case, the weaknesses have been given full attention and steps taken to remedy defects and learn from the experience.

This case was an unprecedented, and hopefully not to be repeated, attempt to bring the JIC into the public domain. No. 10 blandly refuted the charge of meddling in the JIC's drafting processes. But there were over ten messages between No. 10 and the JIC commenting on the draft. I trust we shall not see such behaviour again.

PART FOUR

NON-INFORMATION GATHERING
INTELLIGENCE OPERATIONS

11

SPECIAL OPERATIONS

'Any nation's attempt to dictate to other nations their form of government is *indefensible.*'

President Eisenhower, 1953

'[A] King who alone wished to be absolutely just among the wicked and to remain good among the wolves would soon be devoured along with his flock.'

Pierre-Augustin Caron de Beaumarchais, French spymaster, seeking approval from Louis XVI to covertly aid the Americans in the War of Independence against the British, 1775

'Covert action should not be confused with missionary work.'

Attributed to Henry Kissinger, Secretary of State, 1975

'[C]overt operations have their philosophical and practical difficulties, especially for America. But ... I cannot accept the proposition that the United States is debarred from acting in the gray [sic] area between diplomacy and military intervention.'

Henry Kissinger, former Secretary of State, 1979

'Radio Free Europe and Radio Liberty are public evidence of CIA covert action projects that were successful, [and] served liberal democratic purposes.'

Ray Cline, former DDCI, 1976

'My job is to hold the umbrella above you fellows and catch the crap so you can get on with your operating.'

Richard Helms, CIA operations chief

'The GRU and the KGB helped to fund just about every antiwar movement and organization in America and abroad. ... the GRU and the KGB had a larger budget for antiwar propaganda in the United States than [they] did for economic and military support of the Vietnamese.'

Stanislav Lunev, former Colonel, GRU, 1998

'Our "active measures" campaign did not discriminate on the basis of race, creed, or color [sic]: we went after everybody. ...I had no qualms about stirring up as much trouble as possible for the U.S. government.'

Oleg Kalugin, former KGB general, 1994

This chapter, and the book's remaining chapters, look at clandestine activities that are not concerned with intelligence gathering or assessments. Many Ambassadors and Pro Consuls tended to take a friendly view of the 'funnies', 'irregulars', or 'spooks' on their staff and, if they trusted them, let them get on with it. They were less relaxed, though, about covert action in their parish.

Special Operations aim to affect events. They can be violent, such as the Bay of Pigs invasion discussed in Chapter Nine, or non-violent. In the 1950s and 1960s SIS called non-violent Special Operations 'Special Political Action'. This was an omnibus term covering a wide range of activities including black propaganda, freedom radio stations, intervention in elections, promoting coups d'état, supporting rebels, or any other form of clandestine skulduggery designed to help like-minded friends. This chapter will discuss Special Operations used by the West and by China, and the difficult question of whether the intelligence agencies of democratic states are suited to carrying out these activities.

I had little involvement with classic Special Operations during my official life. But I was on the periphery of such matters when we were seeking, alongside our Malaysian friends, to find ways of persuading Bung Soekarno of Indonesia to desist from his efforts to strangle the infant Malaysia in what was known as the Indonesian Confrontation or 'Konfrontasi'. My suggestions about the use of boats containing concealed naval detachments in the Straits of Malacca to discourage piratical activities by Indonesian patrol boats, or that we might mount a raid to destroy the oil refinery at Balikpapan, were not well received. My only direct participation was an operation to persuade the leaders, whose rebellion in Brunei had been foiled, to surrender. One did, the other did not. I have, however, also observed China's Special Operations over many years.

No serious attempt has been made in the democracies to find the most appropriate home for Special Operations. This is an untidy and highly controversial subject. As the quotations above suggest it is a topic which generates a great deal of heat, although at its height Special Operations never represented more than 3 per cent of the CIA's activities. Although the involvement of the CIA and other states' intelligence agencies in Special Operations today is more often alleged than proved, it retains the ability to cause great controversy among the public, and for state leaders uncomfortable with the idea of one state covertly influencing affairs within another.

Special Operations is not an established term, but it seems bizarre to use generic terms such as 'clandestine action' and 'covert action' for disparate activities that seldom remain secret. These have little in common except that none of them fits tidily into the portfolio of the usual government departments. In the Second World War Britain created a Special Operations organisation under the cover title 'Special Operations Executive' (SOE) and the US created the Office of Strategic Services. In peacetime there is a tendency to look to the intelligence service as a convenient repository for such unconventional, uncomfortable activities, from which traditional departments prefer to withdraw their skirts. In the West, secret services have learnt to look such gift horses in the mouth. It may be flattering to discover that only your agency is thought to have the talents, imagination and enterprise to carry out such operations, and exciting to have an expanded budget. However, experience has taught that Special Operations are more likely than espionage operations to cause problems for Western intelligence services, thereby negating the benefits brought by an expanded portfolio.

Special Operations that go wrong reverberate for years, particularly in the US where some politicians, like Senator Frank Church, chair of the Committee behind the 1976 report into intelligence and the US government, seem almost to make a career out of attacking intelligence. The more successful a Special Operation in bringing about change, the more likely that it will come under public scrutiny. If part of an operation to effect regime change consisted, as it almost certainly would, of funding the opposition parties, the loser would naturally complain of corruption, rigging of the election and so on. It is now public knowledge that the CIA and SIS engineered the 1953 coup that overthrew Mohammad Mossadeq, Iran's democratically elected leader. This adversely affected the reputation of the CIA and its political masters in parts of the world where the US was fighting to win support in the context of the Cold War.

The embarrassment potential is inevitably high in Special Operations. Whereas in espionage cases few will need to know of the operation or the agent's identity, in Special Operations the number who will need to know is much greater, and leakage is therefore more likely. Many people will be involved in planning, training and preparation; there will be risk of seepage and speculation. Plus, a 'blown' Special Operation is likely to cause much more embarrassment than the exposure of even the most spectacular technical operation. Fidel Castro exploited the debacle at the Bay of Pigs to increase his prestige: Cuba was so strong, he claimed, that not even the US could defeat it.[1]

Even in the celebrated case of Commander Crabb's ill-fated underwater reconnaissance of the hull of the Soviet cruiser *Ordzhonikidze* during a state visit to Britain by Khrushchev in 1956, there was only momentary embarrassment. The Soviets enjoyed the opportunity to protest against this unseemly conduct. But their tongues were in their cheeks: they would have had no compunction, had a British cruiser entered a Russian port, in bringing their whole intelligence apparatus into play to uncover her secrets. In private the Soviets were amused. The embarrassment to Britain was not as great as it might have appeared from the newspapers; it was most keenly felt by the confirmed anti-intelligence school, which supports the view that 'gentlemen do not read each other's mail'. In any case, it was small beer compared with the dramatic expulsion, some years later, of over a hundred Russian intelligence apparatchiks, masquerading as diplomats, commercial officers, journalists, and so on in London. That overt blow, struck under the determined leadership of Foreign Secretary Sir Alec Douglas-Home, caused little more than threatening growls from the astonished Soviet Bear, which had grown accustomed to Western determination to avoid confrontation at almost any cost.

The general public may be content that their government should have a secret intelligence service. But there are likely to be more questions about the ethics of Special Operations. Even less violent activities, such as the establishment of a 'free' radio station pretending to be the voice of resistance, sit ill with Western liberal opinion, which hates the idea of states controlling their citizens' access to information. However, there is ample evidence that during the Cold War days of Iron and Bamboo Curtains the residents of the communist dictatorships derived huge comfort from such activities.

It is wrong for governments to dump this ragbag of unconventional subjects on the intelligence services simply because it is too difficult to persuade cabinet ministers and their departments to accept them. If Special Operations are to continue, governments should look at the options rather than merely passing the parcel to intelligence. Take, for example, the peculiarly difficult subject of assassination. Should it be anathemised as something that no civilised country should even contemplate? Or should it be put on the back burner in a small section, keeping abreast of the subject so that in wartime there is a repository of folk memory and experience upon which to draw.[2] Which part of government should be given the lead position for this unattractive task? Regardless of whether democratic states should engage in assassination, their possible use demands that attention be given to where they should be based. This would be an ideal occupation for one or two retired officers with appropriate experience to provide the folk memory. The cost would be negligible; they would be retreads drawing a pension for previous service and motivated by patriotic duty, unsullied by careerism.

It is easy to nominate a home for military Special Operations. Secret services may have relevant language and cultural knowledge, and imagination, but they are chartered and staffed to gather intelligence, not to carry out military operations. It seems sensible to leave the planning and execution of military and paramilitary action, however small, to the military. They have the experience, the skills and the weapons. The responsibility should never be, as it was in the Bay of Pigs case, given to a civilian agency. A grey area exists perhaps in the matter of proxy wars. It may be sensible to give the lead to intelligence for gun running and communications; but military expertise and support must be involved, if only to help to evaluate the capability of the proxy forces they are subsidising.

Examples and Types of Special Operations

Special Operations covers a very wide range of actions. The list below is not exhaustive but reflects one I once drew up for the enlightenment of the Prime Minister of the day about the activities that might be undertaken if the political will required the intelligence services to engage in total war against the enemy. The political masters took note, but only the less violent items were addressed. It can be divided into two broad categories, the non-violent, such as all forms of information work

157

including deception, and the violent, such as paramilitary action and assassination.

Category 1: Non-Violent
    Poison-pen letters
    Rumour mongering
    Leafleteering
    Planting articles
    Distributing seditious literature
    Creating and controlling media outlets
    Establishing 'Free' radio stations
    Feeding information or disinformation to the media
    Deception and disinformation operations[3]
    Funding individuals
    Financing political parties or associations and trade unions
    Bribery[4]
    Psychological warfare
    Black propaganda

Category 2: Violent
    Doctoring ammunition or weapons so that users injure themselves
    Kidnapping
    Rendition (a modern US term for kidnapping in order to exploit a favourable legal jurisdiction)
    Paramilitary operations
    Q Operations[5]
    Training, arming and advising guerrilla movements
    Supporting proxies in military operations
    Assisting in coup d'états
    Assassination

Non-violent types of Special Operations, including propaganda, psy-war and subversion incur relatively small financial costs. DCI Woolsey was certain that the CIA's Freedom Radio had contributed significantly to the collapse of the 'Evil Empire' and East European dissidents, such as the Poles, claimed that the broadcasts played a significant part in the battle. All around the world people listened secretly to the BBC despite the risk of being caught. Perhaps the best proof of the efficacy of 'freedom' broadcasts is provided by the huge effort expended by totalitarian governments to jam foreign broadcasts.

In the 1960s imaginative people in SIS, such as Maurice Oldfield, were working with our liaison partners around the world, helping them to counter Communist subversion and other forms of undesirable activity. But SIS had been smitten with the debilitating fever which followed Philby's defection to the Soviet Union in 1963 and counter-intelligence, seeking out other spies, seemed to take precedence over all else.

MI5 and MI6 were both helping the newly independent nations. The difference between the cultures of the two Services was interesting. MI5, proud of its charter, never paused to wonder what the emerging independent nations thought about their sometimes patronising tone. Christopher Andrew in his official history of MI5 accepts the MI5 view that they played an important role in liaison with the nascent nations that were preparing for independence. Of course they did, but their paternal attitude was not always appreciated. While SIS was in support, MI5 was advising.

Liaison work was an important aspect of Special Political Action. During forty years working in Asia on and off after 1945 I made the most of the opportunity to forge friendships and keep them in good repair. Dividends from my specialisation were substantial and call into question the unsophisticated Whitehall view that ex-colonial officers should never be sent back to their former territories.

The SOE's history provides a useful example of Special Operations being conducted in wartime by a democracy. Fortunately many of the SOE documents, some of which remain classified, have been released into the public domain. The SOE style reflected the nature of the beast; SOE was a rambunctious newcomer set up by Churchill to set occupied Europe ablaze. Neither its members nor its prose style bore much relationship to the papers written by the JIC Secretariat. SOE committees discussed everything and anything, unconstrained by protocol or tradition. They recorded the detail without bothering about what was sensitive and what was not, or genuflections to the *amour-propre* of other officials or concerns about ethics. The papers in the SOE files are rich in operational detail and uninhibited.

The list of SOE activities touched upon in their documents includes the violent and non-violent. At one end of the scale are rumours and itching powder, at the other extreme there are plans for assassination, and in between many ingenious and imaginative ploys such as stoking inflation in Germany. There are proposals to start rumours in their areas.

One 'whisper' started in Switzerland was, within two weeks, the cause of a Vatican condemnation of the practice of using incurables as guinea pigs for medical experiments in Dachau's concentration camp. This gave the Nazis cause to think, although alas, not enough.

Just as the Pearl Harbor disaster provides a rich cornucopia of examples of how not to handle intelligence when a belligerent opponent is squaring up for a fight, so the Bay of Pigs provides rich pickings for the student of the violent category of Special Operations. The CIA was not qualified to organise and direct an amphibious invasion and the US military, although privy to the planning, had no responsibility for the operation.

It is highly likely that canny military personnel would not have proceeded with the operation on the terms laid down by President Kennedy. It was under-equipped, undermanned, insufficiently reconnoitred, and too dependent on unknown factors outside their control, such as the strength of anti-Castro feeling. Successful Special Operations of a military nature have tended to be conducted by Special Forces, not by intelligence agencies.

Two former DCIs, Helms and Colby, both well qualified to make a judgement on the relationship between intelligence and Special Operations, shared their thoughts with me on this topic. The first was a close observer of the Bay of Pigs fiasco, the second was a highly successful Special Operations operator in Vietnam. Neither thought it sensible to give military tasks to the CIA. Helms, reflecting on the Bay of Pigs, wrote in his memoirs that he could not understand the failure by DCI Allen Dulles and his Chief of Operations Richard Bissell, to look more deeply into the facts before undertaking the operation. He could only suppose that their recent brilliant successes with U-2 and satellite imagery programmes had led to a suspension of judgement and collective overconfidence.

In Iraq, Iran and Afghanistan within the last half century Special Operations have played a significant part, but who can say whether without these interventions the result might not have been much the same or, perish the thought, preferable. Such operations are not laboratory experiments. However, as former DCI Woolsey said, '[t]he United States must retain the capability to do something in between sending in the Marines and sending in former President Carter': in other words, a 'third way' between overt military action and negotiations. Politicians who recoil do so for pragmatic not philosophical reasons; Special Operations can open a Pandora's box of unintended consequences.

China and Special Operations

I observed China's Special Operations for thirty years first as a colonial civil servant in Malaya, and later in Whitehall and from British diplomatic missions in Asia. In the 1960s China's intelligence agencies had received instruction in Moscow and had considerable practice in the civil war against the KMT. Like the security agencies of the late Qing period (1644–1911) they had no regard for the niceties of international law when pursuing subversives overseas. Sun Yat Sen, the leading spokesman for revolution in the last years of the Qing Dynasty, was kidnapped and incarcerated in a basement of the Chinese Embassy in London. He managed to throw a note out of his window, which brought his plight to the attention of the British Government, and so he lived to see the overthrow of the Qings. In several well-known instances Chinese operators have enthusiastically followed the kidnapping tradition established by the Qings.

China became notorious for violent and non-violent Special Operations, using agitation and propaganda (known as agitprop), subversion, kidnapping, torture and bribery with a blatant disregard for the normal civilities of relations between nations. Embassies in Beijing were assaulted and foreigners imprisoned without trial. Mao made no attempt to conceal his contempt for the legal, bourgeois, conventions of the West, and did not welcome the diplomatic recognition of his country by Britain. He would have preferred to have no Western diplomats in China observing his activities.

The Chinese campaign in all its forms—propaganda, subversion, bribery, training, arming, and officering guerrilla armies—was expensive, but Mao ruled the Communist Party through terror, and woe betide anyone who challenged his policy. President Liu Shaoqi and Marshal Peng Dehuai, who attempted to restrain Mao's excesses, suffered years of imprisonment, torture and agonising deaths for their impertinence.

China's Special Operations were evident in the American hemisphere. Chinese intelligence officers ranged vigorously from Cuba through Haiti, Brazil, Ecuador, Mexico and Peru. These Chinese efforts were not, however, particularly successful in the face of determined efforts by local counter-intelligence supported by the CIA. Lavish expenditure and hyper activity did not produce the revolutionary results that Mao sought.

Zhou Enlai, the Chinese premier's, public statement that Africa 'was ripe for revolution', although an exaggeration, reflected the Chinese intention to exploit opportunities in newly independent countries abandoned by their erstwhile imperial masters. And the intelligence officers, commanded by Chinese intelligence chief Kang Sheng, exploited every fissure; flattered, entertained sumptuously, bribed, provided arms and training, and even constructed a railway system in Tanzania. Chinese Special Operations activities were extensive and successful.

During my time in China in the early 1960s Beijing was awash with delegations and students from the Third World. The sight of people they perceived to be barbarians being entertained royally while they were on short rations did not please the Chinese people. From the maps which hung on my office walls, the world looked as if it was suffering from measles; they were covered with pins marking the ubiquitous presence of the Chinese Embassies. The New Chinese News Agency, which had offices around the world, might as well have been entitled the New China Intelligence Agency since they made no attempt to conceal the fact that they were engaged in Special Operations. It did not require secret sources to establish the scale and success of their mischief making. For example, Colonel Gao Liang, a Chinese military intelligence officer, performed very effectively as a Head of the NCNA office in Zanzibar. He engineered the marriage of Tanganyika and Zanzibar and masterminded the railway project to link the two countries. Gao Liang's brazen performance, using NCNA cover, included participation in a coup d'état in Zanzibar. Overall, the Chinese performance overseas in the twilight zone of propaganda, subsidy and support was masterly.

Conclusion

As the examples of China and the SOE demonstrate, Special Operations have been used extensively by democracies and totalitarian states. Perhaps wider debate is needed about Special Operations. Views on their acceptability and morality differ widely. In wartime, consciences are likely to be less tender. Governments of democratic states have different views, and operate under different pressures, to those of totalitarian states. The issues of proper training, proper governance and a proper home for Special Operations remain unsolved and under-discussed.

I agree with the views of the realpolitik school: we should retain some option between going to war and negotiation. But history has shown how difficult it is to effect regime change and, even more so, to create an effective alternative government unless, perish the thought, you are prepared to embark on a colonial style, long-term, exercise.

12

DECEPTION OPERATIONS

'[w]e can cause the doomed spy to carry false tidings to the enemy.'

Sun Tzu, 'The Art of War', fifth century BC

'You must search for enemy agents who have come to spy on us. Tempt them with profits, instruct and retain them.'

Sun Tzu, 'The Art of War', fifth century BC

Deception operations are designed to influence events and are heavily dependent on intelligence in every sense of the word. Guesswork about the enemy is unlikely to provide an adequate foundation upon which to create a plausible deception that will fit well with the target's prejudices and preconceptions. The twentieth century is populated with deception operations that have been publicly exposed. The operation widely considered to have been the most successful deception of all time was Operation Fortitude of the Second World War (see below).

Eighteenth-Century Deception

Deception operations have been part of warfare since the beginning of history. During the 1745 Jacobite rebellion, the Hanoverian forces had great difficulty in deciding where to position their three armies in order to intercept the Jacobites because Prince Charlie's staff consistently deceived the government commanders about the Jacobite strength and movements. Their method was simple: they despatched, along routes which the Jacobite Army had no intention of using, small detachments of troops seeking billets and supplies. These activities were faithfully reported by Hanoverian spies, and led the Hanoverians to grossly over-estimate the strength of the Jacobites, as well as deceiving them about the Jacobite plans.

But the Hanoverians knew the value of deception too. In Derby, the most southerly point of the Jacobite march, while the Prince was trying to persuade his commanders that they should continue their advance upon London, a well-dressed, well-mounted, charming and plausible cavalier, calling himself Macdonald, rode in and offered his services as a trooper. He was, in fact, a Hanoverian spy. The Prince and his staff welcomed 'Macdonald' with open arms. He told them that he had just ridden through the Duke of Cumberland's Army at Lichfield: the Duke's army was poised to cut off the Highland army, the Duke of Richmond's army was ready to attack on the right flank and a third army, 8,000 strong, was waiting for them at Northampton. This disinformation was, apparently, accepted by the Prince's staff. To the Prince's fury, his officers decided to abandon their march to London. This case provides a very clear lesson: armies should have a solid counter-espionage department to prevent espionage, capture spies, and ensure security measures are in place that prevent the enemy from collecting intelligence.

The First World War

One of the best-known deception operations in the First World War is attributed to Richard Meinertzhagen, the British Colonel and brilliant and imaginative military intelligence officer. Meinertzhagen prepared a collection of fake papers, including staff appreciations, minutes of meetings and intelligence assessments, all of which implied that the British staff had decided that an attack on Beersheba in Southern Palestine, now part of Israel, was out of the question and that Gaza should be the target for General Edmund Allenby's offensive.

There had been two previous unsuccessful attempts to plant disinformation on the Turks by simulating a careless dropping of official papers, but on both occasions the Turks failed to discover the packages. This time Meinertzhagen cantered off in front of the British lines on what he hoped would be interpreted by the enemy as a foolhardy reconnaissance mission. When the Turkish cavalry galloped out to intercept him, he dismounted, fired a few shots in their general direction, remounted and galloped off dropping a blood stained rifle, equipment and his haversack. This time the Turks found the haversack. As a result of this operation the Turks concentrated on the defence of Gaza and Allenby was able to conquer Beersheba with comparative ease.

The haversack trick was not Meinertzhagen's only contribution to the victory at Beersheba. During the preparation for the battle he had, as part of his Psywar operations, been airdropping messages enclosed in packets of cigarettes on the Turkish Army. Just before the attack on Beersheba, he added opium to the cigarettes, adversely affecting the performance of the Turkish defenders.

Meinertzhagen was always interested in the use of intelligence as an offensive weapon. Twice during his career he imitated the ruthless tactic used by the Chinese General Ts'ao, writing letters to his enemy counterparts, pretending to thank them for their help and enclosing cash as a token of gratitude, knowing that his opponents would almost certainly intercept the letters. But he also excelled in the information-gathering role. His methods included the inspection of the paper used in enemy latrines, which was often discarded staff papers.

A variation on the 'haversack' trick was used in the Second World War to mislead German Intelligence about British intentions in the Mediterranean. In this case, popularly known as *The Man Who Never Was*, or Operation Mincemeat, the medium for deception was a corpse, clothed in the uniform of a British Major, with a briefcase containing planted papers chained to his wrist. The corpse was set adrift off the Spanish coast, and was recovered by the Spanish who passed the case to German intelligence, who swallowed the bait. As a result, the German High Command was seriously misled about the Allied plans in the Mediterranean.[1]

Soviet Deception

Deception has always been a favourite activity of the Russian secret service. Probably the best known case of Soviet deception was Prince Potemkin's alleged late eighteenth-century ploy to convince Catherine the Great that all was well in the Russian countryside by arranging a series of well-painted hoardings along the road, depicting prosperous villages in the distance.

A large scale deception operation, codenamed Trest, involved the creation of the Monarchist Association of Central Russia (MOR), which Felix Dzerzhinsky, a Polish aristocrat turned extreme revolutionary, designed as a means of penetrating Russian émigré circles. Its public aim was to overthrow the Bolsheviks, but the Cheka, the Russian intelligence agency, used MOR as a channel to the principal White Russian émigré organisations. For six-years MOR was seen by Russian émigrés and Western intelligence officers alike as an anti-Communist organisation, but it provided Dzerzhinsky with a cornucopia of counter-intelligence material on Russian anti-Communist exiles. Trest had a large number of members who were genuine anti-Bolsheviks, but who unwittingly betrayed contacts and operations to the enemy as they talked freely to their fellows. Trest also gave Dzerzhinsky a bonus in the shape of identification of the Western intelligence officers who saw the Association as an ideal area for talent spotting and recruitment of agents.

Operation Fortitude

The sheer magnitude, complexity and success of Operation Fortitude far surpasses that of any other deception operation. It was a strategic weapon, which paralysed the Wehrmacht and Hitler when the Allies invaded Normandy. While the Nazis dithered waiting for another attack by our non-existent Second Army Group, the Allies were able to consolidate their bridgeheads. Any major deception operation, depends upon a complex mix of truth and lies. The truth, colloquially known as 'chicken feed', must convince the enemy that they have acquired a reliable source with good access, but not be of such importance that it will give them significant help.

The deception package must be tailored to fit into the enemy's intelligence mosaic and preconceptions. In addition, in wartime there may be a need to provide fake models of weapons and vehicles so that Imint can mislead the enemy as to the strength of your forces. The whole package must be meticulously coordinated; one small slip can cause the enemy to smell a rat. Finally a plausible means must be found to bring the deception to the enemy's attention.

Operation Fortitude met all these requirements. It is impossible to know the number of lives that Fortitude saved by persuading the

German staff that after 6 June 1944, the first day of the Normandy Landings and the day known as D-Day, there were still more than twenty Allied divisions in Britain preparing to launch a second invasion. The German belief in these phantom divisions made a crucial contribution to their dithering, after D-Day, about whether to commit all their tank reserves to the battle for Normandy, or whether to await another blow. By the time Hitler and his Field Marshals had concluded that there would be no second attack, it was too late. The Allies had consolidated their positions.

Fortitude succeeded in persuading the enemy that there were at least twenty Allied Divisions ready to launch a further assault on mainland Europe. On 19 June, two weeks after D-Day, the German ORBAT map still showed more than twelve Allied Divisions in reserve. They had estimated that there were seventy-nine Divisions in Britain before D-Day; the real number was only fifty-two. The High Command had been comprehensively bamboozled by Fortitude.

Members of 49 Division, including myself, were puzzled by the frequency of our moves up, down, around and across Britain in the two years before D-Day. In these years my battalion moved eight times, from Iceland to Llanelli, to the Welsh Border, to Scotland, to Velindre, to Lowestoft, to Southwold and finally to Thetford. This seemed odd in a country suffering severe petrol rationing. No doubt these frenetic movements added to the difficulties of the German staff trying to maintain an up-to-date ORBAT picture.

The Double Cross Operation

Fortitude was supported by Double Cross, a highly successful operation using double agents developed by Britain's Double Cross Committee. Unbeknown to the Germans, Britain had extensively penetrated the network of German agents operating in Britain during the Second World War. The system is described in Masterman's book *The Double-Cross System*: a fascinating read. It underlines the sophistication required to keep so complex a machine working for years, without any hint to the enemy that Britain controlled their agents.[2]

There were three leading agents in the double cross system. The first was agent GARBO, a Spaniard who had once served in General Franco's Army. He offered his services to the Abwehr, and quickly persuaded them that he had an active network of agents working for him in

Britain. It took him longer to persuade MI5 that he was a suitable double agent. By the time that Operation Fortitude was launched, however, GARBO had created twenty-four fictitious sub-agents who, as far as the Abwehr knew, were providing them with intelligence. In fact it was all chicken feed or misinformation.

The second was BRUTUS, a Polish officer, who having been arrested by the Abwehr for espionage, managed to persuade his captors that he had changed his allegiance. He was then despatched armed with radio equipment to Britain and created a mythical dissident Pole to assist him. Agent TRICYCLE, the third of the leading players in the double cross operation, was a Yugoslav lawyer who, as soon as the Abwehr recruited him, offered his services to Britain. Other double agents who had been captured and turned maintained radio contact with their Abwehr case officers.

The following information from the German files show how effectively the system worked.

1944

April 13   GARBO reports by radio that he has seen a lot of troops and vehicles of 49th Division in the Norwich area. [This was chicken feed].

April 14   Germans record that a trustworthy Abwehr report locates the 9th US Infantry Division in the UK. [More chicken feed from GARBO].

May 16   FREAK reports by radio that 15th Division, composed mainly of Scottish troops, has moved to mid-Sussex. [More chicken feed].

May 20   German files record that 15th Division has moved to the Horsham area. [FREAK's chicken feed was noted].

May 31   BRUTUS reports by radio that he will send a series of messages about the (fictitious) First US Army Group (FUSAG). His understanding is that the Allied Expeditionary Forces include FUSAG, commanded by General Patton, and two armies, 1st Canadian, centred on Leatherhead, and 3rd American, location not yet known. [This was false information].

June 6   German files record that, according to a reliable Abwehr message, the forces now in the south of England are organised as two army groups; 21st English [sic] and 1st American. [This was also false information].

June 14   BRUTUS reports that British 2nd Corps is now part of FUSAG and about to move south.

June 16   GARBO reports that US 8th and 9th Air Forces will give heavy support to FUSAG's assault.

June 17   German files record that 2nd English [sic] Army Corps is subordinated to FUSAG, which is in south-east England, and has up to twenty-seven divisions.

June 19   Germans record that a particularly trustworthy source has reported that FUSAG will be supported by strong portions of the heavy bomber force, which suggests an assault on strong fortifications along the middle of the channel coast.

August 31 German ORBAT maps still include FUSAG.

It was not until December 1944 that the German analysts finally decided that there was no danger of a second invasion. The double cross system had been an outstanding success.

Conclusion

Those who question the value of intelligence work should remember Operation Fortitude. Intelligence did in this case save millions of lives and shorten the war. As a soldier who participated in the Normandy battle, I knew nothing of such matters as we fought for weeks against the still powerful German Army. I shudder to think, however, of what might have happened had we not succeeded in our deception and Hitler had allowed his generals to launch all his Panzer reserves against us.

The German records suggest that neither their Sigint nor their Imint contributed significantly to our success. German Sigint intercepted only three messages out of the treasure trove of FUSAG radio messages, so elaborately concocted for their delectation, and the brilliant visual hoaxes created by the Fortitude team were not challenged by aerial photography since the Luftwaffe's operations had become extremely restricted. So it was our fake Humint passed on through the credulous and trusting Abwehr which did the trick.

Many of the examples in this chapter are drawn from World Wars where huge resources were spent on deception operations. Smaller operations, successful or otherwise, in peacetime are much less likely to be revealed in the public records.

13

ASSASSINATION

'[I]f evil men were not now and then slain it would not be a good world for weaponless dreamers.'

Rudyard Kipling, 'Kim', 1901

'In eight months of dramatic investigation, Senator Church had managed to determine that CIA had never assassinated anyone.'

Richard Helms, former DCI, 2003

'[I]n peacetime the assassination of troublesome persons is morally and operationally indefensible.'

Richard Helms, former DCI, 2003

'No person employed by or acting on behalf of the United States Government shall engage in, or conspire to engage in, assassination.'

President Jimmy Carter's Executive Order, 24 January 1978
(an expansion of President Gerald R. Ford's Executive Order of 1976)

'I am against it [assassination] for at least three good reasons: it's against the law of God, it's against the law of man, and it doesn't work.'

Vernon Walters, DDCI, 1976

'The Security Service does not kill people or arrange their assassination.'

MI5 website

WHY SPY?

'If anyone has committed or is planning to carry out terrorist attacks, he has to be hit… It is effective, precise, and just.'

Ephraim Sneh, Israel's Deputy Defence Minister, 2001

There were no doubt cases of murder for political reasons long before there were written records. The Romans were always assassinating their rulers. According to Suetonius, the Roman scholar, eight or even nine of the twelve rulers he described died between 49BC and AD96 at the hands of an assassin. Julius Caesar was one of them. The prize for the assassination which has had the widest and deepest impact on world history should surely go to Gavrilo Princip: his botched, but successful, shooting of the Austrian Archduke Franz Ferdinand was the immediate cause of the First World War, a war which brought the whole of Europe to battle and changed the world. This case reminds us that the consequences of an assassination are unpredictable. For this reason alone—and there are many others—the decision to assassinate an inconvenient ruler should not be taken, however disagreeable the tyrant may be.

Like deception operations and Special Operations, assassination can be conducted by, or on behalf of, intelligence agencies and can make use of intelligence. When non-state actors such as terrorist groups carry out assassinations, just as with their other operations, they are informed by their own intelligence. One of the many risks involved in conducting assassination is that no amount of intelligence can predict the consequences. The 2010 assassination of Hamas official Mahmoud al-Mabhouh in his hotel room in Dubai is believed to have been carried out by Mossad, the Israeli intelligence service. Passports from various western states were used in this operation, bringing about international repercussions that included Ireland's expulsion of an Israeli diplomat from the embassy in Dublin. Various security measures are used to protect state leaders from these kinds of attack, ranging from physical measures such as armoured cars, to counter-intelligence efforts to stop hostile forces from gaining intelligence on state personnel, methods or organisations.

Assassination is a form of special action not favoured in peacetime by democratic governments. In peacetime the extrajudicial assassination weapon has always been anathema among British intelligence services. British scruples did not, however, extend into the Second World War. SOE files, now in the public domain, show that assassination was readily accepted as a potential weapon against troublesome enemy agents, but even in wartime Britain it was not universally accepted. A senior Royal Air Force (RAF) officer refused to authorise the use of RAF planes to drop SOE agents bound for assassination missions in Europe.[1] The charters for MI5 and SIS have never included a licence to kill.

The US too has taken a public stance against dirty tricks of this nature. Founding Father Thomas Jefferson wrote in 1789 that assassination, poisoning and perjury were 'legitimate principles in the dark ages... but exploded and held in just horror in the 18th century.' Nevertheless, in 1916 four assassins were despatched to Mexico by the US Army in an attempt to poison the rebel leader Pancho Villa. Kennedy said publicly in 1961, '[w]e cannot, as a free nation, compete with our adversaries in tactics of terror, [and] assassination'. A Senate Committee set up to study the subject of presidential involvement in assassination produced an ambiguous verdict in 1976 on the degree of knowledge that Presidents Eisenhower, Kennedy and Johnson had possessed about plans to eliminate Cuban leader Castro. Former DCI Helms said in testimony to the Senate, 'I believe it was the policy at the time to get rid of Castro, and if killing him was one of the things that was to be done in this connection, that was within what was expected... no limitations were put on this injunction.'

Yet President Ford issued a directive in 1976 forbidding any US Government employee from engaging in, or conspiring to engage in, assassination operations, and later Presidents have issued similar decrees. However, in May 2011, a US Special Forces operation in Abbottabad, Pakistan led to the death of the Al Qaeda leader Osama bin Laden. His death was celebrated on the streets of the US by delighted crowds.

Lethal force has also been used by the US, and by Britain, to eliminate terrorist leaders in the Middle East by firing missiles from UAVs in complex legal environments. Despite the media attention already paid to the Abbottabad operation and others, there remains scope for further analysis of the relationships between the collection and assessment roles played by intelligence agencies, military action, and political authorisation of the assassination operations.

The Soviets have never seemed bothered about the morality of assassination. They have a long history of brutal secret police. The murder of Bolshevik Leon Trotsky in Mexico in 1940 is, perhaps, the best known of post-Imperial 'out of country' assassinations, but there have been many notorious cases inside and outside the Soviet Empire, where strange and dreadful devices have been used: poison-tipped umbrellas, cyanide-tipped bullets in silenced pistols, and a tube the size of a cigar containing an ampoule of prussic acid designed to spray a victim's face and cause instant death. Oleg Kalugin, ex-KGB, was not coy about assassination in his memoirs: he described the KGB laboratory dedicated to refining and inventing weapons for assassins, and it is widely assumed that the successors to the KGB continue to maintain their skills in this field.[2]

Eisenhower remarked in the context of suggestion that even if any good came from the assassination of Castro, which he doubted, it was immoral and might lead to a chain of assassinations around the world. But SOE had no compunction about assassination in the Second World War. The case of Baron Von Hentig, a German operating in the Middle East in this period, illustrates their philosophy. The only concerns evident in the SOE's war diaries were about repercussions and the opposition of Sir Miles Lampson in Cairo. The war diaries contain many notes relevant to this topic. For example:

… it was understood that Hentig had left on the 26th [of January, 1941] for Damascus and Aleppo. This movement should permit the necessary action to be taken.

… high authorities at Cairo were opposed to any form of assassination which might disturb Syria.

… the High Authorities interested were most disappointed at the failure to deal with HENTIG, and instructed that an attempt should be made to liquidate his assistants KARL RASWEN and MAX VON OPPENHEIM who were in Beyrout.[3]

Conclusion

The word assassination is scarcely mentioned in the British literature. Our intelligence services are no more trained to assassinate than they are to torture. Such training raises moral issues, as does asking or ordering someone to carry out this task in peacetime. And there is no certainty as to what happens afterwards: who will take the assassinated leader's place? Despite this there is evidence to suggest that whilst western democracies have traditionally and quite publicly opposed the use of assassination, their attitudes towards targeting individuals for political and security reasons have altered since 2001. While the legal, practical and moral objections still remain, those whom the west believes are part of the asymmetric threat to their states, and who are located in areas where it is not always clear whether they meet the legal status of 'war zone', are now being specifically targeted with the help of intelligence agencies.

NOTES

PREFACE

1. Herman, Michael, *Intelligence Power in Peace and War*, London: Royal Institute for International Affairs, 1996.
2. Omand, David, *Securing the State*, London: Hurst, 2010.
3. Andrew, Christopher, *The Defence of the Realm: The Authorised History of MI5*, London: Allen Lane, 2009.
4. Jeffery, Keith, *MI6: The History of the Secret Intelligence Service, 1909–1949*, London: Bloomsbury, 2010.
5. Goodman, Michael S., *The Official History of the Joint Intelligence Committee: Volume I: From the Approach of the Second World War to the Suez Crisis*, Oxford: Routledge, 2014.
6. Aldrich, Richard, *GCHQ: The Uncensored Story of Britain's Most Secret Intelligence Agency*, London: Harper Press, 2010.

1. THE MALAYAN EMERGENCY: AN INTELLIGENCE SUCCESS STORY

1. The best all round account of the Malayan Emergency is provided by Tony Short's monumental work, which uses Malayan and British records to provide a broad brush picture of those troubled years. See Short, Anthony, *Communist Insurrection in Malaya, 1948–60*, London: Muller, 1975.
2. Those interested in more detail on SB operations will find them in Stewart, Brian T. W., *Smashing Terrorism in the Malayan Emergency: The Vital Contribution of the Police*, Malaysia: Pelanduk, 2004, and the note on Leng Chee Woh therein.
3. The view that the KMT should not be called in aid against the Communists

and the Commander in Chief's view that the KMT was a worse menace than the Communists was not challenged. The KMT had been the traditional enemy before the war and communist China was not yet seen as a threat.

4. There was no solid basis for this assertion: fortunately for the government the MCP were not clients of any foreign party.

2. VIETNAM: A CAN OF WORMS

1. McNamara, Robert S. with Brian VanDeMark, *In Retrospect: The Tragedy and Lessons of Vietnam*, New York: Vintage Books, 1995, pp. 321–3.
2. Peng, Chin, *My Side of History: Alias Chin Peng*, Singapore: Media Masters, 2003.

3. CHINESE AFFAIRS

1. See Cheng, Nien, *Life and Death in Shanghai*, New York: Grove Press, 1987.

4. THE ORGANISATION AND MACHINERY OF INTELLIGENCE

1. Goodman, Michael S., *The Official History of the Joint Intelligence Committee: Volume I: From the Approach of the Second World War to the Suez Crisis*, Oxford: Routledge, 2014.
2. Penkovsky, Oleg, *The Penkovsky Papers*, London: Collins, 1965.
3. At the time of writing these were, in alphabetical order: Aberystwyth University, Brunel University, King's College London, Staffordshire University, The University of Buckingham and The University of Salford.

5. TYPES OF INTELLIGENCE COLLECTION METHODS

1. There is no simple way of satisfying everyone in the matter of the Romanisation of Chinese words. I have chosen what I think is probably the easiest to remember: Sun Tzu. It is also difficult to agree on translations and there is no agreed standard text for Sun Tzu and the other Chinese military classics. The editions used in this book are: Bin, Sun, Sun Zi, Wu Xianlin, Zheng Tian and Sun Tzu, edited by Wu Rusong, Zhang He and Lin Wusun, *Sun Zi: The Art of War and Sun Pin: The Art of War*, Beijing: China Publishing House, 1995; Sawyer, Ralph D., *The Seven Military Classics of Ancient China*, Oxford: Westview Press, 1993; Zi, Sun, *The Art of War*, London: Hodder and Stoughton, 1981.

6. ASSESSMENT: PROBLEMS AND COMMON FALLACIES

1. Blainey, Geoffrey, *The Causes of War*, New York: The Free Press, 1988 (third edition).
2. Clancy, Tom, *Executive Orders*, London: Harper Collins, 1997.
3. Cockburn, Andrew, *The Threat: Inside the Soviet Military Machine*, New York: Random House, 1983.
4. Personal information from Sir Maurice Oldfield, then Chief of SIS.

7. MORAL DILEMMAS

1. For more accounts of interrogation in the Malayan Emergency see Stewart, Brian T. W., *Smashing Terrorism in the Malayan Emergency: The Vital Contribution of the Police*, Singapore: Pelanduk, 2004.
2. Hoare, Oliver (ed.), *Camp 020: MI5 and the Nazi Spies*, London: Public Record Office, 2000, pp. 57–8, 117–19.
3. Cheng, Nien, *Life and Death in Shanghai*, New York: Grove Press, 1987.
4. CIA, *KUBARK Counterintelligence Interrogation*, July 1963; CIA, *Human Resource Exploitation Training Manual—1983*, 1983, The National Security Archive, http://www2.gwu.edu/~nsarchiv/NSAEBB/NSAEBB122/, last accessed 12 Dec. 2014.
5. CIA, *KUBARK Counterintelligence Interrogation*, July 1963, The National Security Archive, http://www2.gwu.edu/~nsarchiv/NSAEBB/NSAEBB122/, last accessed 12 Dec. 2014.
6. Senate Select Committee on Intelligence, Committee Study of the Central Intelligence Agency's Detention and Interrogation Program, 13 Dec. 2012, http://www.intelligence.senate.gov/study2014/sscistudy1.pdf, last accessed 15 Dec. 2014; Senate Select Committee on Intelligence, Committee Study of the Central Intelligence Agency's Detention and Interrogation Program: Minority Views of Vice Chairman Chambliss joined by Senators Burr, Risch, Coats, Rubio, and Coburn, 20 June 2014, http://www.intelligence.senate.gov/study2014/sscistudy3.pdf, last accessed 15 Dec. 2014.
7. For details of the 1971–2 debate over interrogation techniques in Northern Ireland and further identification of the roles played by heads of service and others, see Newbery, Samantha, *Interrogation, Intelligence and Security: Controversial British Techniques*, Manchester: Manchester University Press, forthcoming (2015).
8. The document is reproduced in Newbery, Samantha, Bob Brecher, Philippe Sands and Brian Stewart, 'Interrogation, intelligence and the issue of human rights', *Intelligence and National Security*, 24, 5 (2009), pp. 631–43.
9. Penkovsky, Oleg, *The Penkovsky Papers*, London: Collins, 1965.

10. For more, see Bunn, Geoffrey C., 'The lie detector's ambivalent powers', *History of Psychology*, 10, 2 (2007), pp. 156–78.

11. Kahn, David, *The Codebreakers*, London: Sphere, 1973; MacLachlan, Donald, *Room 39: Naval Intelligence in Action 1939–45*, London: Weidenfeld and Nicolson, 1968.

12. Masterman, John, *The Double-Cross System: The Incredible True Story of how Nazi Spies were Turned into Double Agents*, New York: Lyons Press, 2000. First published as *The Double-Cross System in the War of 1939–1945* in 1972 by Yale University Press.

13. Hinsley, F. Harry, with E. E. Thomas, C. F. G. Ransome and R. C. Knight, *British Intelligence in the Second World War: Volume 1: Its Influence on Strategy and Operations*, London: Her Majesty's Stationery Office, 1979; Hinsley, with Thomas, Ransome and Knight, *British Intelligence in the Second World War: Volume 2: Its Influence on Strategy and Operations*, London: Her Majesty's Stationery Office, 1981; Hinsley, with Thomas, Ransome and Knight, *British Intelligence in the Second World War: Volume 3, Part 1: Its Influence on Strategy and Operations*, London: Her Majesty's Stationery Office, 1984; Hinsley, with Thomas, C. A. G. Simkins and Ransome, *British Intelligence in the Second World War: Volume 3, Part 2: Its Influence on Strategy and Operations*, London: Her Majesty's Stationery Office, 1985; Hinsley and Simkins, *British Intelligence in the Second World War: Volume 4: Security and Counter-Intelligence*, London: Her Majesty's Stationery Office, 1990.

14. Andrew, Christopher, *The Defence of the Realm: The Authorised History of MI5*, London: Allen Lane, 2009.

15. Chapter Thirteen is devoted to the subject of assassination, including the moral issues it raises.

10. IRAQ: THE INTELLIGENCE IMBROGLIO AND THE BUTLER REVIEW

1. Readers can find a detailed account in the Butler Review and the Hutton Review. See Review of Intelligence on Weapons of Mass Destruction: Report of a Committee of Privy Counsellors, Chairman: The Rt Hon The Lord Butler of Brockwell KG GCB CVO, London: The Stationery Office, 2004, HC 898 (Butler Report); Report of the Inquiry into the Circumstances Surrounding the Death of Dr David Kelly C.M.G., Lord Hutton, London: The Stationery Office, 2004, HC 247 (Hutton Report).

11. SPECIAL OPERATIONS

1. For more on the Bay of Pigs invasion see Chapter Nine.

2. For further discussion of assassination see Chapter Thirteen.

3. See Chapter Twelve.

4. Bribery was a standard weapon for diplomats until the twentieth century. In modern times it may be called by other names, such as 'aid'.

5. This term was used in the First World War to mean operations where the hulls of ships appearing to be innocent and decrepit concealed a naval detachment with a naval gun.

12. DECEPTION OPERATIONS

1. For more on Operation Mincemeat see Montague, Ewan, *The Man Who Never Was*, London: Evans Bros, 1953.

2. Masterman, John, *The Double-Cross System: The Incredible True Story of how Nazi Spies were Turned into Double Agents*, New York: Lyons Press, 2000.

13. ASSASSINATION

1. For more on the SOE see Chapter Eleven.

2. Kalugin, Oleg, *Spymaster: My Thirty-Two Years in Intelligence and Espionage against the West*, London: Smith Gryphon, 1994.

3. SOE War Diaries, 29 January 1941, HS 7/212, The National Archives (TNA); SOE War Diaries, 12 and 5 February 1941, HS 7/213, TNA.

VALEDICTORY

Most of my adult life was spent overseas in Crown Service. Britain was experiencing at first hand regular war, civil war, guerrilla war, colonial administration and postcolonial participation. A very small part of those years were spent in government offices handling government paper. It would be surprising if at the end of such a career my views, perspectives and priorities had not been affected.

Why Spy? has aimed to give a picture of the main elements in a modern intelligence community and the problems they face in seeking the truth in support of the defence of their country. It has discussed the uses, abuses, misunderstandings, weaknesses, strengths, value and limitations of intelligence, and crystallised the rules for good intelligence work into ten commandments. Intelligence alone cannot win a war, but it can be a force multiplier, and can, as in the Malayan case, be a valuable ingredient of victory.

Nonetheless, intelligence, however good, could not have given victory to the US in Vietnam where the basic circumstances assured defeat, not victory. In Iraq the misuse of intelligence contributed to the unfortunate invasion. In many cases, including Pearl Harbor and Afghanistan, it was not intelligence that was needed so much as a much better knowledge of history.

It is theoretically possible to calculate the cost of all our intelligence and security activities, but this is the stuff of accountants. Billions may be spent on security but there is no way of calculating its monetary value. Intelligence is valueless unless the customer puts it to good use.

Those who suggest they know the value of intelligence may only mean that they know that it has been significant. Military commanders sometimes credit intelligence with significant contributions to victory, but intelligence is most often mentioned in the context of failures. The cost of failure could well be the disintegration of society as we know it. I defy anyone to put a price on that.

Although the nature of the threats has changed over time, good intelligence is still a priceless asset. The terrorism we successfully defeated in Malaya was a comparatively primitive affair, and so was the terrorism of the Irish Fenians and other anarchists of the nineteenth century. Those unpleasant activities were small beer compared with the activities of the jihadis of today, equipped with mobile phones and armed with plastic explosives. As the world becomes ever more complex, intelligence continues to be an essential weapon in the armoury of any state seeking to protect its citizens. I salute the intelligence and security officers who, gallantly and doggedly, continue to fight an enemy who are only interested in the rule of law and human rights in so far as such doctrines help them to evade justice.

Valedictories by Ambassadors used to be a fine art; some were strong meat, all were potentially embarrassing. Alas they are no more. This valedictory is of a different sort. This is a farewell after a long life in which seventy adult years were connected in some way with intelligence.

My first Ambassador told me that he liked having an 'irregular' on his staff, and one of my ambassadorial friends told me after reading my autobiography that I had led a much more interesting life than he had. I enjoyed it all immensely, and I hope I made a useful contribution. Intelligence provided me not only with fascinating work, but a hobby for life.

Farewell. I would like to thank all those in the intelligence business with whom I worked over so many years. It was a wonderful club crossing national boundaries. I thank my stars for my involvement in the intelligence world. Friends have asked me whether I would live the same life again. The answer is, 'yes, indeed'. I cannot imagine a more satisfactory occupation, working for Her Majesty, with good company, and my reports sometimes going straight to the Prime Minister and to the President of the US.

I wish my successors well in their sterling efforts to keep British people safe in our turbulent world. They deserve our thanks for their persistence and for their dedication to a profession which may give them job satisfaction but is unlikely to gain them public acclaim.

VALEDICTORY

I leave the last words of *Why Spy?* to Sun Tzu who said, 'what enables the great general to achieve things beyond the reach of ordinary men is foreknowledge… This cannot be obtained by induction or deduction but through spies.'

GLOSSARY AND ABBREVIATIONS

9/11	The terrorist attacks of 11 September 2001
Abwehr	German military intelligence
ARVN	Army of the Republic of Vietnam, or South Vietnam Army
Audint	Audio intelligence
BMA	British Military Administration
BND	German foreign intelligence service
Cabint	Cab or taxi intelligence
Cheka	Communist Russia's espionage and security organisation, 1917–54
Chicken feed	Genuine intelligence used in a deception operation to give the recipients false confidence in the provenance of accompanying, fabricated, intelligence
CIA	Central Intelligence Agency (US)
CINCPAC	Commander in Chief, Pacific Command (US)
CT	Communist-Terrorists (Malaya)
DCI	Director of Central Intelligence (US). The postholder served as Director of the CIA and as national intelligence coordinator. In 2005 this post was replaced by two new posts: Director of the CIA and Director of National Intelligence
DDCI	Deputy Director of Central Intelligence (US). This post was replaced in 2005
DIS	Defence Intelligence Staff (UK)
DNI	Director of National Intelligence (US). This post

	was created in 2005 to oversee the US intelligence community
Docint	Documentary intelligence
Exint	Exile intelligence
FBI	Federal Bureau of Investigation (US)
FUSAG	First US Army Group
GCHQ	Government Communications Headquarters (UK)
GRU	Russian Military Intelligence
Head of Mission	The name given to the most senior representative of a country when stationed in a host country
Humint	Human intelligence
Hunchint	Hunch intelligence
ICBMs	Intercontinental Ballistic Missiles
ICC	International Control Commission
Imint	Imagery intelligence
ISC	Intelligence and Security Committee (UK)
JIC	Joint Intelligence Committee (UK)
KGB	Soviet Union's security, intelligence and police organisation
KMT	Kuomintang, Nationalists China's ruling party until 1949
KUBARK	The cryptonym for CIA Headquarters
MCP	Malayan Communist Party
MI5	The Security Service (UK)
MOR	Monarchist Association of Central Russia
MrBMs	Medium-Range Ballistic Missiles
MSS	Malayan Security Service
NCNA	New China News Agency
NSA	National Security Agency (US)
NVA	North Vietnamese Army
ORBAT	Order of Battle
Osint	Open source intelligence, or overt intelligence
PSB	Public Security Bureau (China)
Psywar	Psychological warfare
RAF	Royal Air Force (UK)
RUC	Royal Ulster Constabulary
Rumint	Rumour intelligence
SAMs	Surface to Air Missiles

GLOSSARY AND ABBREVIATIONS

SB	Special Branch
SCA	Secretary for Chinese Affairs
Security forces	The military and the police
Sigint	Signal intelligence
SIS	Secret Intelligence Service (UK). Also known as MI6
Sitreps	Situation reports
SOE	Special Operations Executive (UK)
SWECs	State War Executive Committees (Malaya)
Techint	Technical intelligence
TNA	The National Archives, London
Trashint	Trash intelligence
U-2	American photo reconnaissance aircraft
UAVs	Unmanned aerial vehicles. Also known as drones
VC	Vietnamese Communists. Also known as the Vietcong
WMD	Weapons of Mass Destruction

SELECT BIBLIOGRAPHY

Aldrich, Richard, *The Hidden Hand: Britain, America and Cold War Secret Intelligence*, London: John Murray, 2001.

────── *GCHQ: The Uncensored Story of Britain's Most Secret Intelligence Agency*, London: Harper Press, 2010.

Andrew, Christopher and Oleg Gordievsky, *KGB: The Inside Story of its Foreign Operations from Lenin to Gorbachev*, London: Hodder and Stoughton, 1990.

Andrew, Christopher, *For the President's Eyes Only: Secret Intelligence and the American Presidency from Washington to Bush*, London: HarperCollins, 1996.

────── *The Defence of the Realm: The Authorised History of MI5*, London: Allen Lane, 2009.

Barker, Nick, *Beyond Endurance: An Epic of Whitehall and the South Atlantic Conflict*, London: Lee Cooper, 1997.

Bin, Sun, Sun Zi, Wu Xianlin, Zheng Tian and Sun Tzu, edited by Wu Rusong, Zhang He and Lin Wusun, *Sun Zi: The Art of War and Sun Pin: The Art of War*, Beijing: China Publishing House,1995.

Blainey, Geoffrey, *The Causes of War*, New York: The Free Press, 1988 (third edition).

Blix, Hans, *Disarming Iraq: The Search for Weapons of Mass Destruction*, London: Bloomsbury, 2004.

Borovik, Genrikh, *The Philby Files: The Secret Life of the Master Spy—KGB Archives Revealed*, London: Little Brown, 1994.

British Army Field Manual, Volume 1, Part 10, *Countering Insurgency*, October 2009.

Bunn, Geoffrey C., 'The lie detector's ambivalent powers', *History of Psychology*, 10, 2 (2007), pp. 156–78.

Cheng, Nien, *Life and Death in Shanghai*, New York: Grove Press, 1987.

CIA, *KUBARK Counterintelligence Interrogation*, July 1963, The National

Security Archive, http://www2.gwu.edu/~nsarchiv/NSAEBB/NSAEBB122/, last accessed 12 Dec. 2014.

CIA, *Human Resource Exploitation Training Manual—1983*, 1983, The National Security Archive, http://www2.gwu.edu/~nsarchiv/NSAEBB/NSAEBB122/, last accessed 12 Dec. 2014.

Clancy, Tom, *Executive Orders*, London: Harper Collins, 1997.

Clarke, Richard, *Against All Enemies: Inside America's War on Terror*, London: Simon and Schuster, 2004.

Cline, Ray, *Secret Spies and Scholars: Blueprint of the Essential CIA*, Washington: Acropolis Press, 1974.

Cline, Ray and William V. Kennedy, *The Intelligence War: Penetrating the World of Today's Advanced Technology Conflict*, London: Salamander Books, 1987.

Cockburn, Andrew, *The Threat: Inside the Soviet Military Machine*, New York: Random House, 1983.

Cocker, Mark, *Richard Meinertzhagen: Soldier, Scientist and Spy*, London: Secker & Warburg, 1989.

Colby, William, *Honourable Men: My Life in the CIA*, New York: Simon and Schuster, 1978.

Colby, William with James McCargar, *Lost Victory: A Firsthand Account of America's Sixteen-Year Involvement in Vietnam*, Chicago: Contemporary Books, 1989.

Comber, Leon, *Malaya's Secret Police, 1945–60: The Role of the Special Branch in the Malayan Emergency*, Victoria: Monash University Press, 2008.

Craddock, Percy, *In Pursuit of British Interests: Reflections on Foreign Policy under Margaret Thatcher and John Major*, London: John Murray, 1997.

Douglas, Hugh, *Jacobite Spy Wars: Moles, Rogues and Treachery*, Stroud: Sutton Publishing, 1999.

Dower, John W., *War Without Mercy: Race and Power in the Pacific War*, New York: Pantheon Books, 1986.

Duiker, William J., *U.S. Containment Policy and the Conflict in Indochina*, Stanford: Stanford University Press, 1994.

Dulles, Allen W., *The Craft of Intelligence*, London: Weidenfeld and Nicholson, 1963.

Elphick, Peter, *Singapore: The Pregnable Fortress: A Study in Deception, Discord and Desertion*, London: Hodder and Stoughton, 1995.

Falkland Islands Review: Report of a Committee of Privy Counsellors, Chairman The Rt Hon the Lord Franks, OM, GCMG, KCB, CBE, London: Her Majesty's Stationery Office, 1983, Cmnd. 8787.

Festinger, Leon, *A Theory of Cognitive Dissonance*, New York: Row Petersen, 1957.

Ford, Harold P., *CIA and the Vietnam Policymakers: Three Episodes 1962–1968*, Langley: Centre for the Study of Intelligence, 1998.

Gates, Robert M., *From the Shadows: The Ultimate Insider's Story of Five Presidents and How They Won the Cold War*, New York: Simon and Schuster, 1996.

Gill, Peter and Mark Phythian, *Intelligence in an Insecure World*, Cambridge: Polity, 2012 (second edition).

Goodman, Michael S., *The Official History of the Joint Intelligence Committee: Volume I: From the Approach of the Second World War to the Suez Crisis*, Oxford: Routledge, 2014.

Gordievsky, Oleg, *Next Stop Execution*, London: Macmillan, 1995.

Griffiths, Samuel B., *The Art of War*, Oxford: Clarendon Press, 1963.

Grose, Peter, *Gentleman Spy: Life of Allen Dulles*, London: Andre Deutsch, 1995.

Haig, Alexander M., *Caveat: Realism, Reagan and Foreign Policy*, New York: Macmillan, 1984.

Helms, Richard and William Hood, *A Look Over My Shoulder: A Life in the Central Intelligence Agency*, London: Random House, 2003.

Herman, Michael, *Intelligence Power in Peace and War*, London: Royal Institute for International Affairs, 1996.

Hinsley, F. Harry, with E. E. Thomas, C. F. G. Ransome and R. C. Knight, *British Intelligence in the Second World War: Volume 1: Its Influence on Strategy and Operations*, London: Her Majesty's Stationery Office, 1979.

———— *British Intelligence in the Second World War: Volume 2: Its Influence on Strategy and Operations*, London: Her Majesty's Stationery Office, 1981.

———— *British Intelligence in the Second World War: Volume 3, Part 1: Its Influence on Strategy and Operations*, London: Her Majesty's Stationery Office, 1984.

Hinsley, F. Harry, with E. E. Thomas, C. A. G. Simkins and C. F. G. Ransome, *British Intelligence in the Second World War: Volume 3, Part 2: Its Influence on Strategy and Operations*, London: Her Majesty's Stationery Office, 1985.

Hinsley, F. Harry and C. A. G. Simkins, *British Intelligence in the Second World War: Volume 4: Security and Counter-Intelligence*, London: Her Majesty's Stationery Office, 1990.

Hoare, Oliver (ed.), *Camp 020: MI5 and the Nazi Spies*, London: Public Record Office, 2000.

Howard, Michael, *Strategic Deception in the Second World War*, New York: W. W. Norton, 1996.

Hughes-Wilson, John, *Military Blunders and Cover Ups*, London: Robinson, 2004.

Jeffery, Keith, *MI6: The History of the Secret Intelligence Service, 1909–1949*, London: Bloomsbury, 2010.

Jones, Reginald V., *Most Secret War*, London: Hamish Hamilton, 1978.

Jones, Reginald V., *Reflections on Intelligence*, Portsmouth: Heinemann, 1989.

Kahn, David, *The Codebreakers*, London: Sphere, 1973.

Kalugin, Oleg, *Spymaster: My Thirty-Two Years in Intelligence and Espionage against the West*, London: Smith Gryphon, 1994.

Keegan, John, *Intelligence in War: Knowledge of the Enemy from Napoleon to Al-Qaeda*, London: Pimlico, 2004.

Kennedy, Robert F., *Thirteen Days: A Memoir of the Cuban Missile Crisis*, New York: W. W. Norton, 1969.

Kessler, Ronald, *Inside the CIA*, New York: Simon and Schuster, 1992.

Knightley, Philip, *The Second Oldest Profession: The Spy as Bureaucrat, Patriot, Fantasist and Whore*, London: Deutsch, 1986.

Lathrop, Charles E., *The Literary Spy: The Ultimate Source for Quotations on Espionage and Intelligence*, New Haven: Yale University Press, 2004.

Laqueur, Walter, *The Uses and Limits of Intelligence*, New Brunswick: Transaction Publishers, 1995 (new edition).

MacLachlan, Donald, *Room 39: Naval Intelligence in Action 1939–45*, London: Weidenfeld and Nicolson, 1968.

MacLaren, Vance V., 'A quantitative review of the guilty knowledge test', *Journal of Applied Psychology*, 86, 4 (2001), pp. 674–83.

Masterman, John, *The Double-Cross System: The Incredible True Story of How Nazi Spies were Turned into Double Agents*, New York: Lyons Press, 2000.

McNamara, Robert S. with Brian VanDeMark, *In Retrospect: The Tragedy and Lessons of Vietnam*, New York: Vintage Books, 1995.

Meijer, Ewout H. and Bruno Verschuere, 'The polygraph and the detection of deception', *Journal of Forensic Psychology Practice*, 10, 4 (2010), pp. 325–38.

Meinertzhagen, Richard, *Middle East Diary, 1917–1956*, London: Cresset Press, 1959.

Misra, Amalendu, *Afghanistan: The Labyrinth of Violence*, Cambridge: Polity, 2004.

Montague, Ewan, *The Man Who Never Was*, London: Evans Bros, 1953.

Newbery, Samantha, *Interrogation, Intelligence and Security: Controversial British Techniques*, Manchester: Manchester University Press, forthcoming (2015).

Newbery, Samantha, Bob Brecher, Philippe Sands and Brian Stewart, 'Interrogation, intelligence and the issue of human rights', *Intelligence and National Security*, 24, 5 (2009), pp. 631–43.

Newsinger, John, *British Counterinsurgency: From Palestine to Northern Ireland*, Basingstoke: Palgrave, 2002.

Office of the Inspector General, CIA, *Report on CIA Accountability with Respect to the 9/11 Attacks*, 2005.

O'Halpin, Eunan, 'British intelligence and the case for confronting Iraq: Evidence from the Butler and Hutton Reports', *Irish Studies in International Affairs*, 16 (2005), pp. 89–102.

SELECT BIBLIOGRAPHY

Omand, David, *Securing the State*, London: Hurst, 2010.

Payne, Ronald, *Mossad: Israel's Most Secret Intelligence Service*, London: Corgi, 1991.

Peceny, Mark, *Democracy at the Point of Bayonets*, Pennsylvania: The Pennsylvania State University, 1999.

Peng, Chin, *My Side of History: Alias Chin Peng*, Singapore: Media Masters, 2003.

Penkovsky, Oleg, *The Penkovsky Papers*, London: Collins, 1965.

Radzinsky, Edvard, *Stalin*, London: Hodder and Stoughton, 1996.

Report of the Inquiry into the Circumstances Surrounding the Death of Dr David Kelly C.M.G., Lord Hutton, London: The Stationery Office, 2004, HC 247 (Hutton Report).

Review of Intelligence on Weapons of Mass Destruction: Report of a Committee of Privy Counsellors, Chairman: The Rt Hon The Lord Butler of Brockwell KG GCB CVO, London: The Stationery Office, 2004, HC 898 (Butler Report).

Richelson, Jeffery T., *A Century of Spies: Intelligence in the Twentieth Century*, Oxford: Oxford University Press, 1995.

Ronge, Maximilian, *The Treachery of Colonel Redl*, London, 1921.

Rusk, Dean, *As I Saw It*, New York: W. W. Norton, 1990.

Ryan, Cornelius, *A Bridge Too Far*, London: Hamish Hamilton, 1971.

Sawyer, Ralph D., *The Seven Military Classics of Ancient China*, Oxford: Westview Press, 1993.

Scarborough, Rowan, *Rumsfeld's War: The Untold Story of America's Anti-Terrorist Commander*, Washington: Regnery Publishing, 2004.

Schlesinger Jnr, Arthur M., *A Thousand Days: John F. Kennedy in the White House*, Boston: Houghton Mieflin, 1965.

Schmidt, Paul and R. H. C. Steed, *Hitler's Interpreter*, Melbourne: Heinemann, 1951.

Senate Select Committee on Intelligence, Committee Study of the Central Intelligence Agency's Detention and Interrogation Program, 13 Dec. 2012, http://www.intelligence.senate.gov/study2014/sscistudy1.pdf, last accessed 15 Dec. 2014.

Senate Select Committee on Intelligence, Committee Study of the Central Intelligence Agency's Detention and Interrogation Program: Minority Views of Vice Chairman Chambliss joined by Senators Burr, Risch, Coats, Rubio, and Coburn, 20 June 2014, http://www.intelligence.senate.gov/study2014/sscistudy3.pdf, last accessed 15 Dec. 2014.

Shackley, Ted and Richard A. Finney, *Spymaster: My Life in the CIA*, Dulles: Potomac Books, 2005.

Short, Anthony, *Communist Insurrection in Malaya, 1948–60*, London: Muller, 1975.

SELECT BIBLIOGRAPHY

Stewart, Brian, 'Winning in Malaya: An Intelligence Success Story', *Intelligence and National Security*, 14, 4 (1999), pp. 267–83.

——— *Smashing Terrorism in the Malayan Emergency: The Vital Contribution of the Police*, Malaysia: Pelanduk, 2004.

Stewart, Rory, *The Places In Between*, London: Picador, 2004.

Strong, Kenneth, *Intelligence at the Top*, London: Cassell, 1968.

——— *Men of Intelligence*, London: Cassell, 1970.

Tenet, George and Bill Harlow, *At the Centre of the Storm: My Years in the CIA*, London: Harper Press, 2007.

Thompson, Robert Smith, *The Missiles of October: The Declassified Story of John F. Kennedy and the Cuban Missile Crisis*, New York: Simon and Schuster, 1992.

Tuchman, Barbara W., *The March of Folly: From Troy to Vietnam*, New York: Knopf, 1984.

Westerfield. H. Bradford, *Inside CIA's Private World: Declassified Articles from the Agency's Internal Journal, 1955–92*, Yale: Yale University Press, 1995.

Whymant, Robert, *Stalin's Spy: Richard Sorge and the Tokyo Espionage Ring*, London: I. B. Tauris, 1996.

Wirtz, James J., *The Tet Offensive: Intelligence Failure in War*, Cornell: Cornell University Press, 1991.

Wise, David and Thomas B. Ross, *The U-2 Affair*, London: Cressel Press, 1963.

Wohlstetter, Roberta, *Pearl Harbor: Warning and Decision*, California: Stanford University Press, 1962.

Zi, Sun, *The Art of War*, London: Hodder and Stoughton, 1981.

INDEX

INDEX

INDEX

INDEX